Romantic Days and Nights®
in San Diego

Help Us Keep This Guide up to Date

Every effort has been made by the authors and editors to make this guide as accurate and useful as possible. However, many things can change after a guide is published—establishments close, phone numbers change, facilities come under new management, etc.

We would love to hear from you concerning your experiences with this guide and how you feel it could be made better and be kept up to date. While we may not be able to respond to all comments and suggestions, we'll take them to heart and we'll make certain to share them with the authors. Please send your comments and suggestions to the following address:

The Globe Pequot Press
Reader Response/Editorial Department
P.O. Box 480
Guilford, CT 06437

Or you may e-mail us at:
editorial@globe-pequot.com
Thanks for your input,
and happy travels!

ROMANTIC DAYS AND NIGHTS® SERIES

Romantic Days and Nights®

IN SAN DIEGO

*Romantic Diversions
in and around the City*

by Alison and Richard Ashton

The
Globe
Pequot
Press

GUILFORD, CONNECTICUT

Cover photo: © David Barnes/The Stock Market
Text design and illustrations by M. A. Dube
Spot art: www.arttoday.com

Romantic Days and Nights is a registered trademark of The Globe Pequot Press.

Library of Congress Cataloging-in-Publication Data
    Ashton, Alison.
        Romantic days and nights in San Diego : romantic diversions
           in and around the city / by Alison and Richard Ashton — 1st ed.
          p.   cm. — (Romantic days and nights series)
        Includes index.
        ISBN 0-7627-0445-4
        1. San Diego (Calif.)—Guidebooks.   I. Ashton, Richard, 1963–.
        II. Title.   III. Series.
    F869.S22A85   1999
    917.94'9850453—dc21   99-15156
                                          CIP

Manufactured in the United States of America
First Edition/First Printing

Contents

The Good Life

Fit for Love

The prices and rates listed in this guidebook were confirmed at press time. We recommend, however, that you call establishments before traveling to obtain current information.

Acknowledgments

WE'D LIKE TO THANK our editors, Laura Strom and Gail Gavert, for their unflagging patience. We are also grateful for the support of many friends and colleagues. In particular, we want to thank Rick Cropp and Barbara Braidwood, Jeanne Ricci, Glenda Winders, Chris Huard, Todd San Jule, Leslee Gaul, and Patricia Walsh.

Thanks, all.

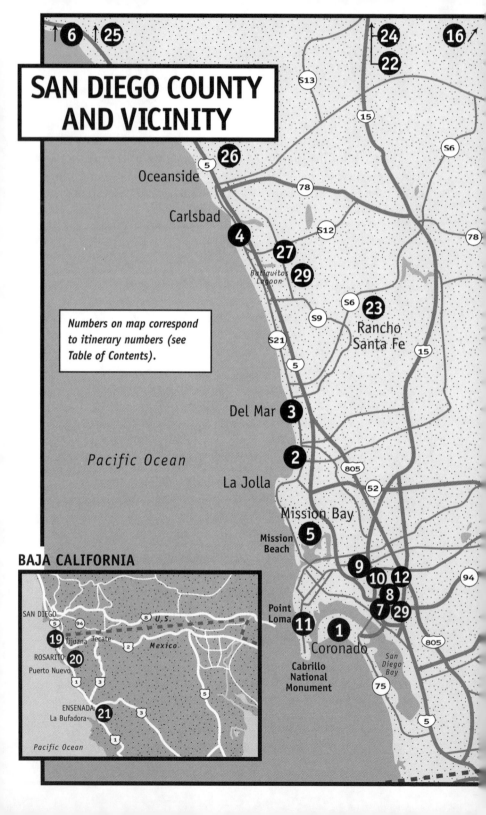

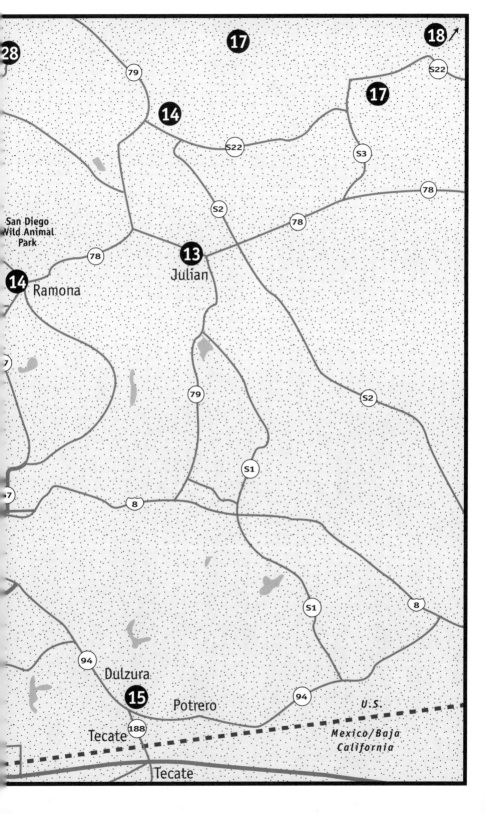

Introduction

JUST HOW ROMANTIC IS SAN DIEGO? Well, this part of Southern California has fostered some of the great romances—real and celluloid—of the twentieth century. It's where Edward, Prince of Wales, met his future wife, Wallis Simpson, in 1920 (or so die-hard romantics believe). Mary Pickford and Douglas Fairbanks frolicked in the horse country of Rancho Santa Fe. And just a stone's throw south of the border, in Rosarito Beach, Leonardo DiCaprio wooed Kate Winslet on the deck of James Cameron's *Titanic*. When you come to San Diego, you can retrace these famous couples' stories, but more important, you can discover your own passion among San Diego's diverse locations.

And that diversity is the key to San Diego as a romantic city. You can return time and again, exploring golden beaches, snow-covered mountain peaks, warm deserts, the bright lights of downtown nightclubs, or the solitude of a cabin in the woods—and still never have the same adventure twice. San Diego has something for every couple, every occasion, every mood.

For all its variation San Diego is a surprisingly compact destination. The promise of a visit here starts from the moment your plane approaches the city's harborside airport. Once you fly over the deserts and mountains of East County, then descend past the Spanish Colonial California Tower of Balboa Park (maybe you even recognize it as Xanadu from *Citizen Kane*), and drop through the high-rises of downtown, you land on a runway that parallels the azure waters of San Diego Bay on one side and swaying palm trees on the other. We think arriving in the city where Charles Lindbergh's *Spirit of St. Louis* was built should be exciting.

And it's only fitting that the city's airport is by the water. Ever since explorer Juan Rodriguez Cabrillo sailed into the harbor and claimed California for Spain in 1542, visitors have been drawn by San Diego's aquatic charms. With 70 miles of coastline, the city still draws much of its identity from the water. San Diego is the home port of naval carriers, cruise ships call weekly, and yachts are moored in marinas off the rocky thumb of Point Loma. San Diego does such a good job of casting its sun-kissed spell that it proudly proclaims itself "America's Finest City." It wears the title especially well on clear winter days, when the ocean is royal blue, the downtown skyline shimmers, and snow-capped mountains tower to the east. As America's seventh-largest metropolis, San Diego has big-city resources but without the urban sprawl, smog, and traffic of other cities.

Whatever mood your romance takes, San Diego can accommodate it in beachfront resorts, intimate B&Bs, elegant yachts, Victorian houses, Spanish Colonial inns, and country farmhouses. Like the people, the city swings to the beat of a multicultural soundtrack. You'll hear the festive, brassy music of mariachi trios in Old Town, the beat of live jazz in the Gaslamp Quarter, Mozart's arias at the San Diego Opera, old-time tunes at the Spreckels Organ Pavilion in Balboa Park, and the pomp and ceremony of navy brass bands on North Island.

Visit San Diego and you won't just fall in love with each other all over again, you'll fall for Southern California's favorite playground, too.

THE ITINERARIES

You can shape your getaway to suit your mood and revel in a different adventure with each visit. If you want a typical, beachy weekend, head to Mission Beach, where you'll find surfers and boardwalk bars aplenty. Seeking more upscale elegance? You'll feel right at home in the gold-plated communities of La Jolla and Del Mar. Or spend a weekend exploring the Victorian mansions and cottages of Coronado, just across the bay from San Diego.

But San Diego is more than beaches. By combining itineraries you can motor from the ocean to the tiny Old West town of Julian, then drop over a mountain pass into the vast solitude of the Anza-Borrego Desert State Park. With more than a half-million acres of hidden canyons and desert badlands ringed by purple mountains, Anza-Borrego is every bit as "San Diego" as the waves crashing on Point Loma's Sunset Cliffs. As you can imagine, the mild year-round climate means San Diego is an alfresco city, so most of the itineraries highlight outdoor activities. Even better, it's a city with no pretenses. You can spend an afternoon Rollerblading around Mission Bay, then dress up a bit to catch a Broadway-bound play in La Jolla. There is so much variety to cover that each itinerary is designed to capture a unique aspect of San Diego.

Each itinerary focuses on a different area, and most are for one- or two-night weekend visits. We've tried to highlight a mix of perennial favorites and spots well off the beaten tourist path to heighten that element of mutual discovery that adds fire to any romance—those little-known neighborhood eateries and one-of-a-kind shops, hotels, and inns that are unique to the area. Some itineraries allow you to explore by foot, while others encourage you to revel in the fun side of SoCal car culture with great driving routes. Getting there is half the fun.

USING THIS BOOK

This book is designed to be a series of self-contained trips. Dip in and taste the flavor of the San Diego you want to sample—we have 29 for you to try. There's a mix for all budgets and tastes, because we don't think you can put a price tag on the romantic qualities of a location. But the right mood and the right couple can find priceless moments to treasure anywhere, whether it's on platinum-card weekends in Rancho Santa Fe (Itinerary 23, Lifestyles of the Rich and Famous) and tony La Jolla (Itinerary 2, Jewel by the Sea) or affordable days cycling down the coast (Itinerary 26, Love Pedals) and exploring Balboa Park (Itinerary 8, Eden in the City). You can easily link two or three itineraries for an extended stay, or pull elements from several to customize your own getaway.

Where possible we've included a couple of options for accommodations—one for a big-ticket stay, the other (every bit as nice) for tighter budgets. Similarly, we consider dining an important element for any romantic adventure. San Diego's restaurant scene has undergone a renaissance in recent years, and that means you'll find more variety and better quality than ever before. These pages include everything from highbrow French cuisine to the best Mexican fare to down-home diners. General price ranges, based on the cost per person for an appetizer, entree, and dessert (not including drinks, tax and tip) will give you some idea of what to expect. "Inexpensive" meals are less than $20 per person, "moderate" is from $20 to $40, and "expensive" indicates more than $40.

GETTING HERE AND GETTING AROUND

There are two airports serving the area. San Diego International Airport at Lindbergh Field and next to downtown is the main point of access. But regularly scheduled flights by most airlines also operate from Carlsbad's Palomar Airport. This airport serves North County, saving you a forty-minute drive for the itineraries in that area. Check with airlines as to flight availability and convenience.

San Diego's public transportation system features the bright red San Diego Trolley and the Coaster train that can take you from Oceanside in the north all the way south to the Mexican border. Trolley fares run from

$1.00 to $2.25. For more information about San Diego's public transit systems, we suggest you call the Transit Store at (858) 233-3004. You can purchase one- to four-day "Day Tripper Passes" ($5.00–$12.00) that allow unlimited access to buses and the trolley system. But like most of Southern California, San Diego is a car town, and having your own wheels is the easiest way to get around. If you need to rent a car, we suggest getting a convertible. Our brilliant year-round weather lets you drop the ragtop and feel the wind in your hair anytime. (It's no surprise that the sporty Mazda Miata was developed in San Diego.)

FOR MORE INFORMATION

San Diego Convention & Visitors Bureau
401 B Street, Suite 1400
San Diego, CA 92101-4237
(858) 236-1212
http://www.sandiego.org

San Diego North Convention & Visitors Bureau
720 North Broadway
Escondido, CA 92025
(800) 848-3336
(760) 745-4741
http://www.sandiegonorth.com

The Best of San Diego

10 MOST ROMANTIC RESTAURANTS

1. Mille Fleurs (Rancho Santa Fe)
2. Top o' the Cove (La Jolla)
3. Trattoria Acqua (La Jolla)
4. Azzura Point (Loews Coronado Bay Resort)
5. Vivace at the Four Seasons (Carlsbad)
6. Cafe Champagne (Thornton Winery, Temecula)
7. Cafe Zucchero (Little Italy)
8. Laurel (Hillcrest)
9. Chez Loma Restaurant (Coronado)
10. Marine Room Restaurant (La Jolla)

5 BEST PLACES TO WATCH THE SUNSET

1. Guy Fleming Trail (Torrey Pines State Reserve)
2. The top of Del Mar Plaza
3. Ferry Landing Marketplace (Coronado)
4. George's at the Cove (La Jolla)
5. Mister A's (Hillcrest)

5 BEST PLACES FOR A FIRST DATE

1. Balboa Park
2. Kensington Grill
3. Brockton Villa Restaurant (La Jolla)
4. Croce's Restaurant & Jazz Bar (Downtown)
5. Extraordinary Desserts (Hillcrest)

10 MOST ROMANTIC LODGINGS

1. Orchard Hill Country Inn (Julian)
2. Bed & Breakfast Inn of La Jolla
3. Heritage Park Inn (Old Town)
4. Rancho Valencia Resort (Rancho Santa Fe)
5. L'Auberge Del Mar Resort & Spa
6. Lake Sutherland Lodge (Ramona)
7. Hotel del Coronado
8. Loews Coronado Bay Resort
9. Brookside Farm Bed & Breakfast Inn
10. Big Cat Cabin (Artists' Loft, Julian)

BEST LODGINGS ON A BUDGET

1. Crystal Pier Hotel (Mission Beach)
2. Les Artistes (Del Mar)
3. Pelican Cove Inn (Carlsbad)
4. Borrego Valley Inn (Anza-Borrego Desert)
5. La Fonda (Rosarito Beach, Baja California)

BEST PLACES TO SMOOCH

1. Alcazar Garden (Balboa Park)
2. Skyfari Aerial Tramway (San Diego Zoo)
3. Spruce Street Suspension Bridge (Bankers Hill)
4. Gondola di Venezia (Coronado)
5. Ellen Browning Scripps Park (La Jolla)

HOTEL DEL CORONADO

America's
Riviera

"Some Like It Hot"
A WEEKEND IN CORONADO

The next day, such a one as may be found only in Coronado in December, we all visited the beach. No finer location could have been found anywhere. . . .
—James Reid, architect of the Hotel del Coronado

CORONADO PROUDLY CALLS ITSELF "San Diego's Enchanted Island." That's half right. Technically, this gorgeous Q-tip of real estate on the stem of Silver Strand State Beach is an isthmus that sits just across the bay from downtown San Diego like a shimmering mirage of the good old days. But San Diego's wholesome, goody-two-shoes little sister is for real. With its well-manicured front yards, lovingly maintained Victorian and Spanish-style mansions and cottages, and Sunday afternoon concerts in the bandstand at Spreckels Park, Coronado manages to retain its turn-of-the-century charm while staying in step with the times—kind of like a groovy barbershop quartet.

Miles of pristine beaches and plentiful cafes make this beguiling slice of small-town America an ideal candidate for a sun-drenched romantic getaway. This two-night itinerary is just an introduction. You'll soon learn why Coronado's cool, salt-laced breezes are a siren call for navy pilots and Arizonans who return to the city every summer to escape the desert heat. Like an old flame, something about Coronado just beckons you back.

PRACTICAL NOTES: Coronado is a year-round destination with cooling ocean breezes and bright, clear days. If you visit during the busy summer season, make hotel reservations well in advance. Fourth of July is particularly festive—this staunchly patriotic military town (the Naval Air Station North Island occupies the north tip of the isthmus) puts on a rousing, old-fashioned celebration complete with a parade down Orange Avenue and naval amphibious demonstrations in Glorietta Bay. The holiday season is a great time, too, when homes and businesses wear Victorian-inspired Christmas finery. The daytime dress code is strictly beach-town casual (don't forget comfortable walking shoes and a bathing suit), with slightly dressier attire for evening. For information about accommodations, dining, and activities, contact the **Coronado Visitors Bureau** (858–437–8788 or 800–622–8300; www.coronado.ca.us). NOTE: **Coronado's area code will change to 935 in June 2000.** Since downtown San Diego is just across bay, you can combine this trip with Itinerary 7, Classic San Diego.

DAY ONE: Morning

Crown City, as residents call it, casts its spell as you drive over the curving blue San Diego–Coronado Bay Bridge that dominates the city's skyline. Ahead the Coronado peninsula lays out its charms with yachts anchored to your right in sparkling San Diego Bay and the signature red roof of the Hotel del Coronado on your left. In the distance the cliffs of Point Loma jut into the Pacific. Since there are two of you, take advantage of the toll-free carpool lane on the far right-hand

Romance
AT A GLANCE

✴ Stay at the grand **Hotel del Coronado** (1500 Orange Avenue; 858–435–6611 or 800–468–5335), the contemporary **Loews Coronado Bay Resort** (4000 Coronado Bay Road; 858–424–4000 or 800–815–6397), or the charming **El Cordova Hotel** (1315 Orange Avenue; 858–435–4131 or 800–229–2032).

✴ Rent a bicycle at **Little Sam's** (1343 Orange Avenue; 858–435–3153) to explore Coronado's neighborhoods of grand oceanfront estates and winsome cottages.

✴ Take a sunset cruise with **The Gondola Company** (858–429–6317) from the Loews Coronado Bay Resort Marina, followed by dinner at the resort's **Azzura Point** (4000 Coronado Bay Road; 858–424–4000).

✴ Join a walking tour of Coronado, starting at the Glorietta Bay Inn, formerly the private estate of sugar magnate John Spreckels.

✴ Relish an intimate dinner at a cozy window table at **Chez Loma Restaurant** (1123 Loma Avenue; 858–435–0061) or rub shoulders with local movers and shakers at the **Prince of Wales Grill** at the Hotel del Coronado.

✴ Enjoy an evening performance at the **Lamb's Players Theatre** (1142 Orange Avenue; 858–437–0600), followed by late-night cocktails and dessert at the Chameleon Cafe's **Lizard Lounge** (1301 Orange Avenue; 858–437–6677).

side. Stay on Third Street, and then turn left onto Orange Avenue, Coronado's main street.

Follow Orange Avenue to your hotel. Coronado offers more than a dozen options, ranging from tiny B&Bs to grand resorts. The 692-room **Hotel del Coronado** (1500 Orange Avenue; 858–435–6611 or 800–468–5335; $205–$650) is the oldest and grandest. Opened in 1888, the "Del" is a National Historic Landmark and one of the oldest wooden structures in the country. As you explore this vast, white-frame Victorian fantasy of red-roofed turrets and stained glass, you won't be surprised that its grand spaces and cozy nooks were the setting for the novel *Bid Time Return*, which was later made into the three-hankie, Christopher Reeve–Jane Seymour tear-jerker *Somewhere in Time*. Coronado's grande dame has hosted fourteen U.S. presidents (President Clinton most recently), international dignitaries, and countless celebrities. Marilyn Monroe frolicked on the beach in front of the hotel in the comedy *Some Like It Hot*. Be sure to check out the Crown Room, right off the lobby. Its crown-shaped chandeliers were designed by L. Frank Baum, author of the *Wizard of Oz* book series. He lived just around the corner from the hotel. With so much history the Del is always bustling with sightseers. For a quieter stay and a little more privacy, request a room in the newer Ocean Tower. It has its own pool and a lovely, quiet stretch of beach.

If you prefer more contemporary digs, **Loews Coronado Bay Resort** (4000 Coronado Bay Road; 858–424–4000 or 800–815–6397; $235–$1,500) is a few miles south of town off the Silver Strand Highway 75. This 438-room resort takes its inspiration from the Mediterranean, with a light, beachy ambience. It occupies a private peninsula overlooking the bay, but you'll find convenient free shuttle service to Silver Strand beach, as well as into town. Ask about the one-night Seaside Rendezvous package when making reservations; it includes a bay-front room, chilled champagne on arrival, and full breakfast served in your room or at the dockside RRR's American Cafe.

 Traveling on a budget? **El Cordova Hotel** (1351 Orange Avenue; 858–435–4131 or 800–229–2032; $75–$295) isn't as lavish as its grand neighbors, but it's redolent of old California charm. Intricate Mexican tile work, wrought-iron decorative gates, and the pleasant burble of a fountain in the lobby impress and soothe. This rambling, salmon-colored adobe complex was built in 1930 and its thirty-six rooms overlook a lush courtyard and a small pool. El Cordova's recently renovated rooms—most on the affordable end of their rate scale—offer quiet solace right on Coronado's main drag.

If your room isn't ready, leave your bags at the front desk and rent a pair of beach cruiser bikes to get your bearings. Both the Hotel del Coronado and the Loews have bike rentals, or rent your wheels at **Little Sam's** (1343 Orange Avenue; 858-435-3153). Beach cruisers are $5.00 per hour, including locks and maps.

While you pedal around town, arrange a small surprise for your sweetheart. Ask your hotel to deliver an arrangement of fresh flowers to the room, or call **Ye Olde Flower Shoppe** (El Cordova Shops; 858-435-2241) and ask owner Bob Creel to create a dramatic display of fresh-cut blooms.

Coronado's quiet residential streets are ideal for lazy bike rides, but for an overview of the island, ride past the Del and turn right on Ocean Boulevard. On the left are the white-sand dunes of Central Beach, but the mansions of "Millionaire's Row" across the street will catch your eye, too. They're an intriguing architectural mix of mock Tudors from the early 1900s to Spanish Colonial haciendas from the 1920s. Bike along the waterfront to Naval Air Station North Island, and then follow the residential streets around the perimeter of the island. Eventually you'll pick up a bike path just before reaching the Ferry Landing Marketplace. Before the San Diego–Coronado Bay Bridge was built in the 1960s, residents and visitors reached the island by ferry from downtown San Diego. A pedestrian ferry still plies the bay, but the old landing's real cachet is its smashing views of downtown San Diego. This is a good spot to stop and refuel yourselves with an iced cappuccino from a waterfront espresso cart.

DAY ONE: *Afternoon*

LUNCH

If it's lunchtime and you're at the Ferry Landing Marketplace, enjoy San Diego's skyline view from a patio table at **Peohe's** (1201 First Street; 858-437-4474; moderate). But all that pedaling can really work up a good thirst; you may want to sample the suds at the island's microbrewery, **Coronado Brewing Company** (170 Orange Avenue; 858-437-4452; inexpensive). Order a wood-fired pizza or a couple of burgers to accompany a pint of home-brewed ale or lager.

After lunch pick up the bike path from the Ferry Landing as it curves past dinky Tidelands Park, under the bridge, and around the Coronado Municipal Golf Course. From there you'll follow Glorietta Boulevard back to your hotel.

Epic Encounter?

It was the event of the decade when the young Prince of Wales, later England's King Edward VIII, visited the Hotel Del Coronado in 1920. Among the nearly 2,000 guests at a reception in the prince's honor was Wallis Warfield Spencer, wife of Naval Air Station North Island's commanding officer and later the scandalous, twice-divorced Wallis Simpson. Was this the first meeting between the prince and the woman for whom he abdicated the throne sixteen years later? No one knows for sure, since some reports say Wallis was out of town on the night of the big shindig, while others speculate she was among the many women waiting on the receiving line to curtsy and shake the young dandy's hand. Wallis's Coronado home has since been moved to the hotel grounds and is now the Duchess of Windsor Cottage, a prime spot for weddings and private parties.

DAY ONE: *Evening*

Unwind with a relaxing sunset gondola cruise with **The Gondola Company** (Loews Coronado Bay Resort Marina; 858–429–6317). Your SoCal gondolier isn't likely to serenade you in Italian, but he will be dressed in a traditional Venetian gondolier's black-and-white striped shirt, and he'll play a tape of recorded Italian opera music while steering you through the quiet canals of the Coronado Cays. If the breeze picks up, as it often does late in the day, snuggle under a blanket and absorb the view.

Hour-long cruises are $62 per couple, including an antipasto salad, wineglasses and a bucket of ice (you provide the vino, which can be picked up at Loews RRR's Market).

DINNER

Provided you didn't gorge on the goodies served in the gondola, you'll be ready for dinner after the cruise. Upstairs at the Loews is the award-winning **Azzura Point** (858–424–4000; expensive). This dining room has a warm, luxurious ambience—a touch of old Venice meets North Africa with a decor of golds, apricots, and leopard-print accents—that invites you to linger over the ever-changing seasonal menu. Sink into a plush banquette and prepare to enjoy. The pan-seared John Dory with fennel is a winner; so is the lobster risotto. Pacific Coast oysters with iced sake mignonette may or may not be a bona fide aphrodisiac, but they'll at least satisfy an adventurous culinary yen.

DAY TWO: *Morning*

Following last night's sybaritic feast, a morning walk along the beach will help jump-start the day. You may spot a herd of Navy SEALs jogging past. After a stroll through the sand, with the salt-scented ocean breeze in your face, you'll be ready for breakfast.

BREAKFAST

Return to the hotel for a leisurely *petit déjeuner*, or walk to one of the many cafes in town. For coffee and a fresh-baked goodie, join the local crowd at **Coronado Bakery** (1206 Orange Avenue; inexpensive). Satisfy bigger appetites at **Clayton's Coffee Shop** (979 Orange Avenue; inexpensive), where traditional diner-style breakfast is served in a retro-1950s setting complete with tabletop juke boxes.

 Coronado Touring (858-435-5993) offers an easy, ninety-minute stroll through the island's historic neighborhoods for $6.00 per person. Tours depart on Tuesday, Thursday, and Saturday mornings at 11:00 A.M. from the music room of the **Glorietta Bay Inn** (across the street from the Hotel del Coronado). Formerly the mansion of San Francisco sugar magnate John D. Spreckels, the inn offers a glimpse of how the upper class lived in the early 1900s. Spreckels came to San Diego after the massive earthquake of 1906 in San Francisco. He considered his Italianate estate overlooking Glorietta Bay to be a modest affair—much like the grand "cottages" of Newport, Rhode Island—but he became a key figure in early San Diego (the huge organ in Balboa Park was his gift to the city). Tour guide Gerry MacCartee offers a lively commentary as she leads you through the grounds of the Hotel del Coronado, and then down Ocean Boulevard to point out some of the grander mansions, including one Spreckels built as a wedding gift for his son and daughter-in-law.

DAY TWO: *Afternoon*

LUNCH

Head to the cool, shady courtyard of the El Cordova Hotel, where you'll find **Miguel's Cocina** (1339 Orange Avenue; 858-437-4237; inexpensive). Choose a table on the patio (it's heated year-round) for a leisurely lunch of Mexican fare. If you're not too hungry, just order a generous portion of nachos and a couple of beers or margaritas.

After lunch you could browse through stores along Orange Avenue. If you need reading matter for the beach, pop into **Bay Books** (1029 Orange Avenue; 858-435-0070) for a fine selection of international magazines and the latest best-sellers. Need a new bikini or a pair of trunks? You'll fit in with the local surf rats in beachwear from **Emerald City Surf 'N' Sport** (1118 Orange Avenue; 858-435-6677) or **Island Surf** (1009 Orange Avenue; 858-435-1527).

Spend the rest of the afternoon lounging on Coronado's excellent beach, where you can watch a steady parade of locals strolling on the sand and maybe glimpse dolphins playing in the surf. Staying at the Del or the Loews? They'll provide beach towels, chairs, umbrellas, and even boogie boards for riding the waves. If you stay at El Cordova, remember to bring your beach gear.

DAY TWO: *Evening*

DINNER

Make reservations for an early dinner at **Chez Loma** (1132 Loma Avenue; 858-435-3770; expensive) or the **Prince of Wales Grill** (in the Hotel Del Coronado; 858-522-8496; expensive). Occupying a restored Queen Anne cottage, Chez Loma is a longtime local favorite where chef-owner Ken Irvine serves a seasonal menu of contemporary French dishes—fresh fish, chicken, pork, and beef—all with his signature sauces. Try the roast duckling with a medley of cherry-lingonberry, green peppercorn, and burnt orange sauces. An extensive wine list features a mix of French and California vintages. The recently remodeled Prince of Wales Grill is a cozy, elegant spot that pays homage to the hotel's regal past (with old photos on the wall, a snappy retro-deco decor, and Cole Porter tunes on the piano) while serving up a revamped menu of Continental/California cuisine.

After dinner it's a short stroll to catch the evening performance at the **Lamb's Players Theatre** (1142 Orange Avenue; 858-437-0600). This year-round repertory company stages first-rate productions, usually a mix of West Coast premieres and revivals.

Hopefully you didn't splurge on dessert after dinner, because you'll find plenty of tempting treats at the hip **Lizard Lounge** in the **Chameleon**

Cafe (1301 Orange Avenue; 858-427-6677; inexpensive). Also owned by Ken Irvine, this eatery features a fusion of Southwestern and Pacific Rim cuisine in a casual, contemporary setting. Irvine offers terrific after-theater happy hour specials on Fridays and Saturdays. Gorge on dessert, or just sip one of his signature chocolate martinis.

DAY THREE: *Morning*

BREAKFAST

Order breakfast from room service and enjoy your last morning in Coronado.

Not in a hurry to return home? Schedule a tee time at the **Coronado Municipal Golf Course** (2000 Visalia Row; 858-435-9485). The eighteen-hole beauty features views of the Glorietta Bay Marina, the Del, and the Coronado Bridge. Greens fees are $20 per person to walk the course; $32 with a cart.

Or spend more time on the water and rent a sailboat or tandem kayak ($20 per hour) from **Action Sports** (858-424-4466) at the Loews Coronado Bay Resort Marina.

FOR MORE ROMANCE

Lounging on the beach in the late afternoon, you'll see navy aircraft coming in for a landing at Naval Air Station North Island. Coronado's romance with aviation is nothing new—North Island's airstrip dates back to the earliest days of flight. Charles Lindbergh took off from that airstrip in the *Spirit of St. Louis* in 1927 on the first leg of his historic flight across the Atlantic. You can see the base with **Old Town Trolley Tours** (858-298-8687; $20 per person) on Friday mornings; trips depart from the Ferry Landing Marketplace.

Jewel by the Sea
La Jolla's Lavish Charms

HE SOUTH OF FRANCE MAY HAVE the Cote d'Azur, but Southern California has La Jolla. This wealthy seaside enclave shares a lot with its Gallic sister. Palm tree–lined streets, expensive boutiques, well-heeled residents and a sparkling coastline make La Jolla a touch of Cannes in California, but with better beaches. Indeed, La Jolla wears an air of exclusivity—this 10-carat jewel glitters and knows it. Today it's home to Nobel Prize–winning scientists, artists, and other notables. And, yes, it's still a favored getaway for the rich and beautiful. You just might find yourselves rubbing shoulders with Barbra Streisand, George Will, and Gillian Anderson, which should give you some idea of La Jolla's diverse appeal.

PRACTICAL NOTES: La Jolla is a year-round retreat, but if the two of you want to swim its clear waters, plan a trip in the late summer when water temperatures are at their highest all year: 72 degrees. Bring a mask and snorkel so you can see the underwater life of La Jolla Cove. Be sure to bring comfortable walking shoes, since this village is best explored by foot. To experience the contrasting flavors of San Diego's beach life, combine this itinerary with Itinerary 5 to Mission Beach and Bay.

DAY ONE: *Afternoon*

Start your perfect La Jolla getaway at the quintessentially "LJ" **La Valencia Hotel** (1132 Prospect Street; 858–454–0771 or 800–451–0772; $235–$1,200). This pink, Mediterranean-style grande dame has presided over busy Prospect Street since 1926. Judging by the cars that keep the hotel's corps of valets hopping, it's also a favored hostelry and watering hole among the rich and famous. The hotel's one hundred rooms have been nicely spruced up over the last few years. Some have a refreshing, blue-and-white beachy decor. Rooms overlooking the water are premium, but worth the extra pennies for the entrancing view.

The **Bed & Breakfast Inn at La Jolla** (7753 Draper Avenue; 858–456–2066 or 800–582–2466; $90–$250) is a pleasant hideaway a few blocks from the busy shops and restaurants of Girard Avenue and Prospect Street. The only sound you'll hear is the gentle "thwack" of tennis balls rallied at the La Jolla Recreation Center courts across the street. Designed by architect Irving Gill in 1913, the inn is another historic treasure—once a private home occupied by composer John Phillips Sousa and his family in the 1920s. Today, its sixteen rooms are individually decorated, and several have fireplaces. Request the Holiday room—its king-size canopy bed, oversize whirlpool tub, fireplace, and cozy sitting area make it popular for intimate celebrations. Another winner is the Gill penthouse. It has a deck overlooking the water.

LUNCH

Even if the two of you choose to stay at the bed-and-breakfast inn, a lazy lunch at La Valencia is not to be missed. After all, the Spanish Colonial–style pink palace is the hub of local activity. The cool, shady Mediterranean Patio offers light entrees and first-rate people-watching. This is where you'll see La Jolla's Chanel-clad society matrons lunching. If it's chilly, you can always retreat to the adjacent dining room (request a table overlooking the cove). "La V's"

Romance
AT A GLANCE

✶ Stay at the intimate **Bed & Breakfast Inn at La Jolla** (7753 Draper Avenue; 858–456–2066) or the tony **La Valencia** (1132 Prospect Street; 858–454–0771). Both offer prime locations in the heart of the village.

✶ Check out the undersea life at **Stephen Birch Aquarium-Museum** (2300 Expedition Way; 858–534–3474).

✶ Hike along the clifftop **Guy Fleming Trail** in Torrey Pines State Reserve (858–755–2063). This easy path affords one of the most spectacular views on the coast.

✶ Have a candlelight dinner in the gazebo at **Trattoria Acqua** (1298 Prospect Street; 858–454–0709).

✶ Enjoy a morning stroll along Coast Walk, followed by breakfast at the **Brockton Villa Restaurant** (1235 Coast Boulevard; 858–454–7393).

✶ Explore La Jolla's sea caves on a late afternoon kayak trip with **Aqua Adventures** (858–272–0800 or 800–269–7792).

✶ Catch a Broadway-bound performance at **La Jolla Playhouse** (2910 La Jolla Village Drive; 858–550–1070).

recently remodeled Whaling Bar has a dark, clubby feel—it's a popular watering hole among local movers and shakers. Actors Gregory Peck and Mel Ferrer often retreated to the bar after performing at La Jolla Playhouse in the 1940s.

Spend the rest of the afternoon strolling along La Jolla's streets. Specialty boutiques and galleries line Prospect Street and Girard Avenue—perfect for window shopping and maybe a little spending, too. For more culture, drop by La Jolla's **Museum of Contemporary Art, San Diego** (700 Prospect Street; 858–454–3541; admission $4.00). Even if modern art isn't your cup of tea, the museum's light-filled exhibit space is worth the visit, and you'll certainly be captivated by the views from the side of the museum that faces the ocean. The permanent collection features works by the likes of Andy Warhol and Frank Stella, while changing exhibitions highlight new talent. Also check out the whimsical sculptures in Edwards Garden. A few doors up from the museum is **John Cole's Book Shop** (780 Prospect Street; 858–454–4766), a delightful spot to browse for a new read. Meander through the book-filled rooms, which offer titles ranging from current best-sellers to out-of-print specialty books.

By late afternoon, you'll be ready to return to your digs. Wine and cheese are served at the inn—a good time to mingle with other guests, or just relax by yourselves on the patio. Or just head to the casual ocean terrace at **George's at the Cove** (1250 Prospect Street; 858–454–4244) for a sunset cocktail and appetizers.

DAY ONE: *Evening*

DINNER

Some of San Diego's fanciest eateries are in La Jolla, but for your first evening make reservations at the popular and casually elegant **Trattoria Acqua** (1298 Prospect Street; 858–454–0709; moderate). The tables in the warmly lit dining room are nice, as are the patio tables, but reserve one in the romantic gazebo. It's a quiet spot to enjoy entrees like lobster ravioli or funky pizzas created by local notables.

After dinner, stroll along the waterfront and watch the waves crash on the rocks. Nightlife in La Jolla is pretty low-key, but definitely check out the live entertainment (piano tunes, maybe a small band) at **La Sala** in La Valencia Hotel. Overstuffed chairs, cozy couches, and hand-painted wood beam ceilings lend the room an old-world charm and make it a popular after-dinner spot with the locals.

DAY TWO: *Morning*

Join the locals and start your day together with a constitutional along the water. Follow Coast Boulevard, past Children's Pool (where the seals are just rousing themselves for the day) to La Jolla Cove. Continue up the hill, keeping an eye out for the entrance to a blufftop trail through the pine trees. This short hike takes you past grand oceanfront houses—some of Southern California's choicest real estate—and smashing views of La Jolla Bay.

BREAKFAST

End your morning stroll at the **Brockton Villa Restaurant** (1235 Coast Boulevard; 858–454–7383; moderate), across the street from La Jolla Cove. Built in 1894, this charming white bungalow was one of La Jolla's earliest beach cottages. Most people wait for a table on the deck overlooking the water, but the cozy dining room is a sweet retreat, too, especially at a table by the fireplace inlaid with pearly abalone shells. The menu is a mouthwatering roundup of steamed eggs, omelettes, and fresh-baked goodies. If the sea air isn't enough to wake you, order a Keith Richards. That's four (count 'em!) shots of espresso topped with cinnamon-spiced Mexican hot chocolate.

La Jolla is world renowned for its picturesque beaches and crashing surf. After breakfast, why not make the most of it and spend the rest of the morning at La Jolla Cove? The sandy beach is tiny, even when the tide is out, so choose your spot on the grass under the shade of the palm trees at Ellen Browning Scripps Park. Named for La Jolla's patron matriarch, the park is a haven for serious swimmers, who come to paddle in the cove's calm, protected waters, as well as scuba divers and snorkelers. Slip

Literary La Jolla

Long a favorite with artists and academics, La Jolla has attracted its fair share of writers. Raymond Chandler lived here in the 1930s and 1940s. The hamlet turns up as Esmeralda in his noir mystery Playback. In the late 1960s, Tom Wolfe turned a sharp eye on the beach town's teen surfers in The Pumphouse Gang. You can see their hangout at Windansea Beach, as well as the Windansea surf shack, which was recently made a historic landmark—the first to pay homage to California's surf culture. Theodore Geisel, beloved as Dr. Seuss, penned his keen children's verse in a hillside aerie. His fable about snobbery, The Sneetches, is rumored to be based on the social mores of the La Jolla Beach and Tennis Club.

on your masks and fins, if you brought them, and slither into the water to check out the sea life. Just few yards offshore you'll see the kelp beds for which San Diego's coast is famous. Residents include bright-orange garibaldis and dinky leopard sharks (they don't bite). You may even spot a stingray flapping along the ocean floor.

DAY TWO: *Afternoon*

LUNCH

La Jolla isn't all haute cuisine eateries. One of the best-loved spots is **Jose's Court Room** (1037 Prospect Street; 858–454–1891; inexpensive), where locals gather to sample Mexican fare and sip margaritas. Nab a window seat so you can watch the passersby on busy Prospect Street while you share a quesadilla or maybe nosh on nachos—ideal après-beach fare.

After lunch hop in the car for a short drive to the small but beautiful **Stephen Birch Aquarium-Museum** (2300 Expedition Way; 858–534–3474; admission $7.50). Part of the world-famous Scripps Institution of Oceanography, the aquarium is as enjoyable for its primo location as for its collection of underwater residents. If your morning didn't include a dip in the cove, this is your chance to meet the local sea life. If you did go snorkeling, a trip to the aquarium will help you identify what you saw. Unless one of you is an amateur Jacques Cousteau, you can probably cruise through the exhibits in just over an hour. Be sure to check out the Southern California tanks in the Hall of Fishes, where you'll see tiny smoothhound sharks, stingrays, and writhing moray eels. The floor-to-ceiling Kelp Forest tank is hypnotic as you watch shoals of graceful silvery ocean whitefish flutter past. Perhaps prettiest of all is the languid underwater ballet of the luminescent moon jellyfish. They look like puffs of taffeta floating in the dark water. Also step out to the Preuss Plaza to investigate an artificially created tide pool that houses local marine plants and animals. The view of the Pacific is pretty enticing, too.

From the aquarium it's a short drive to the 1,700-acre **Torrey Pines State Reserve** (Torrey Pines Park Road, just off North Torrey Pines Road; 858–755–2063). Ask the ranger for directions to **Guy Fleming Trail**, a short blufftop path that affords spectacular views of the Pacific. To your right is the coast of Del Mar, to your left are the rocky cliffs of La Jolla's rugged coastline. Scan the water for dolphins playing in the surf—this is one of their favorite coastal hangouts.

Hardier souls will want to schedule a kayak tour with **Aqua Adventures** (858–272–0800 or 800–269–7792). This local outfitter offers paddling excursions to explore the sea caves off La Jolla Cove ($55 per person, including equipment) from May through October. It's a view of La Jolla few people see. November through January, you can schedule a whale-watching journey (also $55 per person).

DAY TWO: *Evening*

DINNER

Plan to dress up for dinner at the **Marine Room Restaurant** (2000 Spindrift Drive; 858-459-7222; expensive). This longtime institution at the end of La Jolla Shores beach was a bit frayed around the edges until Chef Bernard Guillas came on board in 1995 and revamped the menu with zippy French flair and first-rate ingredients. Reserve a table by the window—the waves crash against the building at high tide. That kind of drama alone makes an evening at the Marine Room worthwhile.

You'll find a different kind of drama—or comedy or musical—at **La Jolla Playhouse** (2910 La Jolla Village Drive North; 858-550-1070). The playhouse, originally established by local boy Gregory Peck and his pals in 1947 and reopened at the University of California San Diego campus in 1983, has developed a national reputation for an intriguing mix of new works and revivals. Some productions, such as Pete Townsend's "Tommy," debuted at the playhouse before hitting Broadway.

DAY THREE: *Morning*

A late night deserves a lazy morning. Enjoy a late breakfast at your hotel. If you're staying at La Valencia, opt for room service. Staying at the B&B? Reserve a patio table for breakfast.

FOR MORE ROMANCE

Need to recover from your active weekend? Schedule spa treatments in the serene confines of the ultra-trendy **Chopra Center for Well Being** (7630 Fay Avenue; 858-551-7788 or 888-424-6772; www.chopra.com). Under the direction of wellness guru Dr. Deepak Chopra, the center offers massage, facials, and other treatments based on the ancient Indian system of healing called *ayurveda*. Services range from $55 to $180.

Where the Turf Meets the Surf

OLD DEL MAR

*J*UST A TWENTY-MINUTE DRIVE NORTH OF SAN DIEGO is the picturesque—and aptly monikered—seaside town of Del Mar. Bing Crosby crooned that it's "where the surf meets the turf" in his song commemorating the famous racetrack that he helped found. But Del Mar is more than just a summer racing season venue. It's one of the most charming, least spoiled waterfront communities in Southern California.

Del Mar is an exclusive area where million-dollar mansions rub shoulders with modest seaside bungalows. It's home to plenty of upscale shops and restaurants yet maintains a low-key village ambience. Facing the Pacific Ocean, Del Mar resides on a gentle slope that drops down to sandy beaches. When the tide is out, you can walk the entire length of Del Mar's Dog Beach all the way south to La Jolla Shores, a good 10 miles south. Del Mar has stunning cliffs from which to watch dolphins frolic in the surf or, in winter, spot migrating gray whales.

PRACTICAL NOTES: Del Mar is compact, so you won't need a car to get around. The annual racing season at the Del Mar Racetrack and Fairgrounds, which runs from the end of July to the beginning of September, usually means that the town is booked solid with high-roller gamblers, forcing hotel rates through the roof and making restaurant reservations almost impossible. Unless a visit to the track is on your agenda, it's best to avoid Del Mar during this time of year. It's easy to combine this weekend getaway with Itinerary 23 to the gold-plated community of Rancho Santa Fe.

About the Authors

ALISON ASHTON IS A SAN DIEGO NATIVE, and British ex-pat Richard Ashton has called San Diego home since 1986. Their travel features are syndicated by Copley New Service, and their work has appeared in *Walking, Weight Watchers Magazine,* Microsoft's San Diego Sidewalk.com, *Meetings in the West,* and *The Meeting Professional.* While they suffer frequent bouts of wanderlust, they always love to return to the beaches, mountains, and deserts of their home town.

DAY ONE: *Late Morning*

In the heart of Del Mar check in at the elegantly appointed **L'Auberge Del Mar Resort and Spa** (1540 Camino del Mar; 858-259-1515; $239-$359). This luxe resort is discreetly off Del Mar's main drag, so it offers privacy and a prime location near shops and restaurants. L'Auberge has 120 deluxe rooms, all with a private balcony or patio, yet it doesn't have a "big" feel. The management has an excellent track record for catering to romantic requests. Concierge Nancy Hirsch has done everything from scattering rose petals and running an aromatherapy bath for an evening surprise to arranging a cruise on a private yacht.

 Couples traveling on a budget should make reservations at **Les Artistes** (944 Camino del Mar; 858-755-4646; $60-$155). Several years ago, local architect Sulana Sae-Onge took the dilapidated Old Village Motel and transformed it into a delightful hideaway. This pink-adobe inn has twelve rooms; for a special getaway, book one of the designer rooms. Each is named after a different artist and carries the appropriate decor. The Mexican-themed Diego Rivera room is the largest and has an ocean view. The Japanese-inspired Furo room has an inviting soaking tub.

TIP: You don't have to stay at L'Auberge Del Mar to use its spa. Whether you stay at L'Auberge or Les Artistes, book a spa treatment when you make reservations.

Romance AT A GLANCE

✳ Indulge yourselves at **L'Auberge Del Mar Resort and Spa** (1540 Camino del Mar; 858-259-1515). Traveling on a budget? Check out **Les Artistes** (944 Camino del Mar; 858-755-4646), a pink-adobe charmer where every room is different.

✳ Unwind at the spa at L'Auberge Del Mar. A $6.00 Spa Pass buys you unlimited use of all the spa and sports facilities (a great bargain).

✳ Pick up a volume of love sonnets at **Esmeralda Books & Coffee** (1555 Camino del Mar; 858-755-2707).

✳ Enjoy a spectacular ocean view while lunching on the sun-drenched patio at **Enoteca del Fornaio** (1555 Camino del Mar; 858-755-8639).

✳ Browse through the high-end boutiques at **Del Mar Plaza** (1555 Camino del Mar; 858-755-8639). Need a little something to stoke the romantic fire? The luxurious European lingerie at Neroli is unlike anything you'd find at the neighborhood Victoria's Secret.

✳ Book a sunset hot-air balloon safari with **Skysurfer Balloon Company** (1221 Camino del Mar; 858-481-6800).

Treatments at the spa are a worthwhile indulgence. Prices start at $42 for half-hour massages and facials. If you just want to relax in the steam room and sauna, buy a $6.00 Spa Pass. It allows you to use L'Auberge's pools, tennis courts, and exercise facilities, too.

You may just want to sit around the pool at L'Auberge, sipping cool drinks while basking in the sunshine. But if you're up for it, lace up your walking shoes and check out Del Mar.

DAY ONE: *Afternoon*

Just a block to the west of L'Auberge is the beach at Del Mar. You can stroll down, walk in the surf, and observe the surfers jockeying for a good spot in the waves. As you walk north you'll pass beachfront homes with million-dollar views. Lucille Ball and Desi Arnaz once lived in one of these homes. So did actor Pat O'Brien.

A walk into town brings you to an eclectic mix of stores—not your usual tourist knickknack shops, but an intriguing mix of surf shops, cigar bars, New Age bookstores, and tony clothing and housewares boutiques. Across the road from L'Auberge is the **Del Mar Plaza** (1555 Camino del Mar), a sun-drenched, modern-day marketplace filled with one-of-a-kind shops and plenty of potential lunch spots.

Where the Surf Meets the Turf

Ever since it opened in 1937, the Del Mar Racetrack and Fairgrounds (Jimmy Durante Boulevard at Via de la Valle) has drawn plenty of star power. The Del Mar Turf Club was founded by crooner Bing Crosby and his pal actor Pat O'Brien. Along with residents Jimmy Durante and Desi Arnaz, they made Del Mar a chic retreat for the Hollywood set in the 1930s, '40s and '50s. The racetrack got a much-needed face-lift in 1993 and, yes, the July through Labor Day racing season still draws plenty of famous people, who hang out at the exclusive Turf Club. The grandstand seats are fun, too. Whether you bet or not, cheering your pony on can be thrilling. The first race kicks off at 2:00 P.M. daily.

LUNCH

The plaza's top level affords a smashing view of the ocean, and you'll want to pull up a pair of brightly painted Adirondack chairs to soak it in. You won't have to move far for a lunch—**Enoteca del Fornaio** (1555 Camino del Mar, in Del Mar

Plaza; 858-755-8639; moderate) is the casual outdoor extension of the Italian restaurant, Il Fornaio. There you can share a pizza or focaccia sandwich, washed down with a nice Chianti from the extensive wine selection. Wrap it up with a cappuccino and espresso served by one of the laid-back Italian waiters and, for a moment, you just might think you're vacationing on the Cinqueterra.

After lunch, head to **Esmeralda Books & Coffee** (1555 Camino del Mar; 858-755-2707), a terrific small bookshop tucked at the back of the plaza. The knowledgeable staff are always happy to make recommendations, whether you want the latest best-seller or a volume of love poems. Of course, you also can do some shopping of a more personal nature. For her, **Neroli** (858-792-2883) specializes in luxurious lingerie imported from Europe, or you can find some chic togs for both of you at **Peaches en Regalia** (858-792-7400) or **Gerhard** (858-792-9709).

A signature sight in Del Mar is the giant hot-air balloons gently floating in air every afternoon. Here is a romantic excursion that'll take your breath away, especially at sunset. **Skysurfer Balloon Company** (1221 Camino del Mar; 858-481-6800) offers packages that'll show you spectacular bird's-eye views of Del Mar, Rancho Santa Fe, La Jolla Valley, and the endless Pacific. Hour-long sunset flights are $135 per person Monday through Friday, $145 on Saturday and Sunday, including on-board refreshments and hors d'oeuvres after the flight. Conveniently, excursions depart from Skysurfer's office on the town's main street.

DAY ONE: *Evening*

Having explored the town, either by foot or from the sky, you might want an early cocktail before preparing for dinner. Drop in at the casual **En Fuego Cantina & Grill** (1342 Camino del Mar; 858-792-6551; inexpensive). This Mexican restaurant has a lively bar where you can sip a margarita and get the lowdown on local haunts from the residents.

DINNER

Pacifica Del Mar (1555 Camino del Mar; 858-792-0476; moderate to expensive) is the perfect setting for a special dinner. True to its name, Pacifica Del Mar specializes in fish dishes with Pacific Rim flair. The Japanese clam chowder offers a twist on the well-known favorite. For a spicy dish try the horseradish-encrusted mahimahi with wasabi mashed

potatoes. The grilled, blackened catfish is a favorite, as the charbroiled New York steak marinated in beer and served with blue cheese. The burnished copper decor of the dining room makes a warm and inviting place to relax, while the outdoor patio offers an ocean view. Pacifica Del Mar is a local hot spot, so don't forget to make reservations for a table for two with that view.

Staying at L'Auberge Del Mar? Ask the management to leave a bottle of chilled champagne and chocolate-dipped strawberries in your room as a delightful après-dinner nightcap. Or just relax under the stars while sipping a cognac at Enoteca del Fornaio.

DAY TWO: *Morning*

You've probably noticed by now that Del Mar is a popular spot with triathletes, runners, and cyclists, who often gather at the local cafes and coffeehouses after a morning workout. If all these hard bodies have inspired you, start the day with a run along the water or a workout at L'Auberge's small gym. Afterward, just throw on some sweats and walk up the street for a well-deserved breakfast—you'll fit right in.

BREAKFAST

Stratford Court Café (1307 Stratford Court, 858–792–7433; inexpensive) is one of Del Mar's best-kept secrets. Located just off the busy main strip, it's where the locals in the know, as well as celebrities passing through town, hang out. The hideaway cafe is an add-on to a Tudor-style house, and all seating is at tables on an outdoor deck. Breakfast is served from 6:30 A.M. to 4:00 P.M. daily. Try the black bean and scrambled egg burrito for something a little different.

FOR MORE ROMANCE

Quail Botanical Gardens (230 Quail Gardens Drive; 760–436–3036; $5.00 per person) is just ten minutes north of Del Mar in the beach town of Encinitas. This 30-acre Eden is devoted to plants from regions around the world with climates similar to Southern California. Head to the lavender-scented Mediterranean Gardens and claim a private, tree-shaded bench with a view of the ocean, or stroll to the Overlook Pavilion, which stands guard over native coastal canyon shrubs. Or drench your eyes with the sight of the lush ferns and waterfalls in the Tropical Rainforest Exhibit. On your way out, stop by the on-site nursery to take home your own cutting from paradise.

A Village By the Sea
CARLSBAD

FULL OF THE QUAINT SPOTS THAT MAKE FOR AN IDYLLIC romantic retreat, Carlsbad offers a quiet escape from the more heavily
trafficked tourist spots farther south. In this delightful hamlet
contrasts comfortably coexist. Colorful fields of flowers overlook the
Pacific, funky antique stores are just up the road from an upscale new outlet mall, and taco shacks share the neighborhood with a trendy wine
country eatery.

PRACTICAL NOTES: Officially called the Village of Carlsbad By-the-Sea,
it's a beach community where high season is spring and summer. Even then,
it never appears crowded. Any time of year, casual attire is in order. The most
colorful time is March and April, when the commercial Carlsbad Flower
Fields are ablaze in a rainbow of hues. Don't forget your camera to document
your stroll through the fields, which are open to the public.

DAY ONE: *Afternoon*

Arriving in Carlsbad village you're at once in the center of a thriving beach
community as casual and laid-back as any in Southern California. A special place to stay is the **Pelican Cove Inn** (320 Walnut Street;
888–735–2683; $90–$180). This Cape Cod-style hostelry is off the beat-
en path on a residential street, yet it's just 200 yards from the beach and a
stone's throw from restaurants and shops. Each of the inn's eight rooms is
individually decorated and named after a Southern California beach
town. All boast welcome amenities for a romantic getaway—gas fireplaces,
down comforters, and fresh flowers. The La Jolla room has a wonderful
vaulted ceiling, an inviting bay window, and a spa tub.

While your room offers plenty of reasons to stay inside, the village of Carlsbad is just steps away. A gentle afternoon's stroll into town means you can enjoy a brief respite in one of the many coffee shops. **Kafana Coffee** (3076 Carlsbad Boulevard; 760–720–0074; inexpensive) is a fine spot for watching the world go by while sipping lattes. From there amble up Carlsbad Boulevard to Carlsbad Village Drive, which is lined with dinky antiques shops, used-book stores, and vintage clothing boutiques.

During March and April the **Carlsbad Flower Fields** (Palomar Airport Road at I–5; 760–930–9123; $4.00 per person) are in full bloom and open to visitors, who swarm among the blossoms like happy bees. The fields offer fifty acres of commercial nurseries ablaze in a riot of purple, yellow, red, and orange. A stroll through the endless rows of blossoms is a walk you'll remember, if only for the heady floral perfume.

Having walked through the flowers and the town, you've probably worked up a thirst and need a little restoration. Stop by the **Carlsbad Mineral Water Spa** (2802 Carlsbad Boulevard; 760–434–1887) to sample the natural spring waters that give Carlsbad its name. The waters have the same mineral content as those found at the famous spas in Karlsbad, Czech Republic.

If you need more pampering, take a dip in the mineral baths ($30) or schedule a body treatment. Treatment packages, including a mineral bath soak with aromatherapy, a facial, and a full hour massage start at $120.

If you thought that *The English Patient* and *Out of Africa* were romantic, be sure to schedule a sunset flight with **Barnstorming Adventures** (located at McClellan-Palomar Airport; 800–759–5667). They'll take you on a flight in one

Romance AT A GLANCE

✳ Book a room at **Pelican Cove Inn** (320 Walnut Street, 888–735–2683), an eight-room B&B tucked away on a quiet residential street.

✳ In spring the commercial **Carlsbad Flower Fields** (Palomar Airport Road at I–5; 760–930–9123) are ablaze with color and open to the public. Bring your camera to take snapshots of your honey among the blooms.

✳ Take "the cure" and sip the local mineral water at **Carlsbad Mineral Water Spa** (2802 Carlsbad Boulevard; 760–434–1887).

✳ Re-enact your own "Out of Africa" romance with a sunset ride in a biplane booked through **Barnstorming Adventures** (800–759–5667).

✳ Romance over a rare vintage and dinner at **Bellefleur Winery & Restaurant** (5610 Paseo del Norte; 760–603–1919).

✳ Browse through the antique stores in the village of Carlsbad or do some serious shopping at the upscale **Carlsbad Company Stores** outlet mall.

✳ Borrow beach chairs and towels from the inn to spend the morning at the beach.

of their biplanes soaring above Carlsbad and the Pacific. Staggeringly beautiful scenery will leave you proclaiming, "I had a farm in Africa." A twenty-minute flight is $98 for two, or reserve an hour-long "Sunset Snuggler" for $298 per couple. The "Snuggler" flies you up and down the coastline as the sun sinks into the horizon and the skies turn red. The plane then climbs higher so you can witness the sunset a second time.

DAY ONE: *Evening*

DINNER

Located at the northern end of the Carlsbad Outlet Mall is the **Bellefleur Winery & Restaurant** (5610 Paseo del Norte; 760–603–1919; moderate). The cavernous building has roomy, cushioned booths in the Vineyard Grill Room for an intimate dining experience, or you can sit out on the patio if the weather is pleasant. While waiting for your table, take in a tour of the winery itself and marvel at the giant wooden vats. You may want to take home a bottle, since you can't find Bellefleur's wine anywhere else. The menu offers some wonderful salads, outstanding grilled salmon in grape leaves, pan-seared sea bass, and an outrageous hanger steak with horserad-ish mashed potatoes, to name just a few stellar items. Not hungry for a major meal? Head to Bellefleur's Vintner's Bar for a tasty selection of "Small Plates" nibbles and gourmet pizzas.

DAY TWO: *Morning*

Like so much of San Diego, Carlsbad has a large and dedicated commu-nity of surfers, who rise before dawn to take advantage of the morning tides. From the parks overlooking the beaches, you can watch them vie with dolphins to catch a wave.

Back at the inn breakfast is part of the romantic package. An assortment of pancakes, Scotch eggs, breakfast quiches, and fruit is served in the parlor, on the bougainvillea-shrouded gazebo in the back garden, or in the privacy of your room. That should set you up for a long, lazy morning at the beach. Carlsbad's beaches are just south of the village itself. South Carlsbad State Beach runs down the main coastal road to the Carlsbad Power Station (a can't-miss local landmark). Farther south are Ponto Beach, Carlsbad State Beach, and finally Carlsbad City Beach. The innkeepers will be happy to

lend you beach chairs and towels. You provide the sunscreen and trashy novels.

DAY TWO: *Afternoon*

LUNCH

Overlooking the beach the **Harbor Fish South** (3179 Carlsbad Boulevard; 760-729-4161; inexpensive) is a fish-and-chips shack offering terrific fish tacos. While the décor is strictly just-off-the-beach casual in the extreme, it's a nice spot to hang out. The server will ask if you want one or two tacos. Don't be fooled—one of these babies, filled with a huge filet of fish, is plenty.

If you want to indulge an urge to spend, a trip to the **Carlsbad Company Stores** (5620 Paseo del Norte; 760-804-9000) is a must. Here you'll find dozens of outlet stores for major name-brand retailers, such as Barneys New York, Donna Karan, Polo Ralph Lauren, North Face, and Kenneth Cole. Once your dogs start barking from all that shopping, the two of you can relax over a malt at the retro-50s **Ruby's Diner**. If shopping is a "for her" activity, then on a quid pro quo basis, the "for him" treat would be a pilgrimage to the **Callaway Golf Company** (2285 Rutherford Road; 760-930-8687), manufacturers of the famous Big Bertha clubs.

FOR MORE ROMANCE

If you just have to try out those new clubs you bought at Callaway, book a tee time on the challenging links at **Four Seasons Resort Aviara** (7100 Four Seasons Point; 760-603-6800). Save your pennies, though: greens fees are a rich $165 per person, including a cart.

For more shopping hop on the Coaster train for a ten-minute ride south to Solana Beach and spend a few hours exploring Cedros Street's home-design boutiques. This is a great spot to pick up a nifty new tchotchke to feather your nest at home.

Sun, Surf and Sand

MISSION BEACH AND BAY

*I*F THE TWO OF YOU LONG FOR THE CAREFREE DAYS of college spring break, consider this weekend escape. From Crystal Pier at the north end to the South Mission Jetty 2 miles south, Mission Beach has all the youthful exuberance of a permanent spring break. Strolling down the beachfront boardwalk during San Diego's endless summer, you'll witness a sea of young hardbodies (of both genders) sunbathing, playing volleyball or just kickin' back and savoring the cool breeze off the Pacific. All this takes place under the watchful gaze of real-life California lifeguards, not the oversiliconed wannabes of *Baywatch* fame. While pretty young things congregate on the sand, Mission Beach cheerfully welcomes everyone into the fold, from aging Hell's Angels to young families. You'll feel at home, too, especially after joining the crowds that gather along the seawall every evening in hopes of glimpsing the fabled "green flash" as the fat old sun dips below the horizon. Feel free to just do your thing—whatever that is, you'll just add to the local color.

Mission Beach is chock-full of vacation rentals, great bars, and a variety of restaurants. And best of all, it's one of San Diego's less-expensive spots to visit. The community really has two sides. There's the popular Pacific-facing side, and then across the road Mission Bay offers both calmer waters and less-crowded sands. It's a nice antidote to the teeming crowds on the beach side.

PRACTICAL NOTES: Mission Beach is a popular destination for locals and tourists alike. Peak summertime often means standing room only on the beach and parking lots full to capacity. Better stake your claim on the sand early in the day during the peak months of June through September. At Christmastime (usually the second Saturday of December) you can wrap up and watch the festive Festival of Lights on Mission Bay as local boat owners

parade through the water, with their craft flickering with elaborate light displays. Any time of year, the dress code here is strictly beach casual, though you may want to pack slightly dressier clothes for dinner. Be sure to pack the sunscreen. Even in winter, the rays can be bright. If you want, combine this trip with Itinerary 2 to La Jolla, Mission Beach's more polished, debutante cousin.

Romance
AT A GLANCE

* Reserve a cottage at the **Crystal Pier Hotel** (4500 Ocean Boulevard; 858–483–6983 or 800–748–5804), a groovy local landmark where the crashing waves sing a soothing lullaby.

* Catch a thrill with a nostalgic ride on the **Belmont Park Giant Dipper**, one of the oldest wooden roller coasters in the country.

* Rent bicycles or in-line skates at **Hamel's** (704 Ventura Place; 858–488–5050) and join the locals on the boardwalk. Miles of bike paths make it easy to explore.

* Have dinner at romantic table No. 7 (beside the fireplace) or on the patio at the **Lamont Street Grill** (4445 Lamont Street; 858–270–3060).

* Visit Shamu, San Diego's most famous resident, at **SeaWorld Adventure Park** (500 SeaWorld Drive; 858–226–3901). For a really special experience, sign up for the park's Dolphin Interaction Program.

DAY ONE: *Morning*

You really can't start the day too early in Mission Beach. Between surfers catching waves at dawn and joggers treading up and down the boardwalk, this is as much a community of early risers as late-night party animals. One of the best-kept secrets on Mission Beach is the **Crystal Pier Hotel** (4500 Ocean Boulevard; 858–483–6983 or 800–748–5894; $85–$275). Most local vacation rentals offer oceanfront views, but this treasure goes one better—guests "sleep over the ocean." While the pier is open to pedestrian traffic during the day, guests have it to themselves at night. The pier has been a local landmark since 1927, and you'll feel special as you drive (a privilege reserved for guests) through its great white entrance gate to park in front of your cottage. Choose from among twenty-nine cottages that have been refurbished in recent years in the hotel's trademark white-clapboard and blue-shutter Cape Cod color scheme. The cottages have hardwood floors, simple, beachy decor of wicker furniture dressed in gingham or indigo denim, and private patios with lounge chairs and umbrellas enclosed by a white picket fence. For maximum privacy, book a unit on the far end of the pier.

If your cottage isn't ready, drop your bags at reception and join the local parade of humanity. Mission Beach bustles early in the morning.

Strolling along Oceanfront Walk or on the sand, you can enjoy the crashing waves of the Pacific while joggers and in-line skaters exercise up and down the boardwalk.

BREAKFAST

Just across from the Crystal Pier Hotel, the smell of hot coffee and cinnamon rolls wafts from **Kono's Surf Club** (704 Garnet Avenue; 858-483-1669; inexpensive). There you can enjoy some first-rate people-watching as you sip a cappuccino.

There are a number of options for a hearty breakfast along Mission Beach, from Kono's on the north end to **Homies Cinnamon Rolls** (735 Santa Clara Place; 858-488-2354; inexpensive), south of the hotel. For a taste of something strikingly different, there is the wonderful **Mission Café and Coffeehouse** (3795 Mission Boulevard; 858-488-9060; inexpensive to moderate). The menu is an eclectic fusion of Mexican and Asian flavors combined with traditional American fare. Whimsically garnished with fruit puree swirls, plates of the blueberry pancakes look too pretty to eat—almost. Or start the day with the *Papas loco,* a spicy and hearty mélange of potatoes, black beans, tortillas, and peppers. At first glance the Mission looks a bit grungy, but therein lies its charm. Try to nab one of the cozy window booths.

Exploring Mission Beach is easy enough. Visit the giant faux castle facade of **Hamel's** (704 Ventura Place; 858-488-5050) to equip yourselves with either in-line skates or bicycles. From there you can discover the nooks and crannies of both sides of the beach and bay. The waterfront homes are an architectural testament to Mission Beach's anything-goes attitude—grand, million-dollar villas sit next to frat-house hangouts like cheerful odd couples.

DAY ONE: *Afternoon*

Looking for a thrill before lunch? Halfway down the boardwalk you'll encounter Mission Beach's historic roller coaster at **Belmont Park** (3190 Mission Boulevard; 858-488-1549). For $3.00 each, the two of you can take a trip back in time as you rattle around on the old wooden Giant Dipper. It was given National Historic Landmark status in recent years as one of the oldest surviving wooden roller coasters in the nation. At night it's illuminated with fairy lights as thrill seekers clatter along the tracks under the stars.

LUNCH

Walk a block inland and you're on Mission Boulevard, which is a veritable restaurant row offering endless choices for lunch. **Saska's** (3768 Mission Boulevard, 858–488–7311; inexpensive) is a longtime fixture of the Mission Beach scene and is famous for its steaks and fresh fish dishes. On a bright summer day, sit on the open rooftop to take in the view. A few doors down, **Guava Beach** (3714 Mission Boulevard, 858–488–6688; moderate) offers delicious lobster tacos in a cozy beach bar setting.

The Roaring Twenties

Mission Beach was developed by sugar tycoon and San Diego landowner John D. Spreckels, who envisioned a grand "Venice of America." Well, that never came to pass, but remnants of Spreckels' dream remain at the Mission Beach Amusement Center, the centerpiece of which was the Giant Dipper roller coaster in Belmont Park and the Plunge swimming pool. Long gone, the Dance Casino was once a hot nightspot in the 1920s, though parts of its old, ornate facade still stand in Belmont Park.

Crossing Mission Boulevard brings you to the bay side. Significantly quieter than the beach side, Mission Bay stretches in a long 10-mile loop. Boating enthusiasts moor their sailboats, motorboats, and jet skis in the water along Bayside Walk. The calm water may entice you to rent a tandem kayak at the **Catamaran Hotel** (3999 Mission Boulevard; 858–488–1081) or **Southwest Kayaks** (2590 Ingraham Street; 619–222–3616). Rentals are $15–$16 per hour or $25–$45 for a half day.

DAY ONE: *Evening*

DINNER

Mission Beach and its adjoining neighborhood, Pacific Beach, have no shortage of rowdy collegiate nightlife. Beach bars and nightclubs are everywhere. For a perfect romantic dinner you'll want to make reservations at the **Lamont Street Grill** (4445 Lamont Street, 858–270–3060; moderate to expensive). Hidden behind a wall of ivy, the restaurant is an intimate

hideaway with an outstanding menu and wine list. Whatever your mood, hearty steaks, fresh seafood, or light pastas will make both of you happy. Do share two of the house specialties: baked Alaskan halibut and a filet mignon drizzled with stone-crushed mustard butter. The patio offers delightfully romantic seating for a balmy summer night. In the fall or winter you'll want to sit inside in one of the cottage's wings, preferably near the roaring fireplace (ask for table No. 7). Tip: Dressy-casual is the attire for here.

Before bed, take advantage of the fact that Crystal Pier is open only to hotel guests at night. You'll enjoy plenty of privacy for a moonlight promenade over the water. Once you retire, let the crashing waves lull you to sleep.

DAY TWO: *Morning*

BREAKFAST

World Famous (711 Pacific Beach Drive, 858–272–3100; inexpensive) offers an oceanfront view for breakfast, serving traditional American fare. For big appetites, order the "World Famous Wipeout," a massive repast of three eggs and three buttermilk pancakes, plus ham, bacon, or sausage and potatoes or refried beans. Feeling more adventurous? Order the Chilaquiles—corn tortillas simmered in spicy ancho chili sauce and topped with two eggs, sliced avocado, and sour cream. Either way it's a perfect start to a day in which you might take in Mission Bay's major tourist attraction, **SeaWorld Adventure Park** (500 Sea World Drive, 619–226–3901; admission $38 per person).

Built on the south shores of Mission Bay, for many visitors, SeaWorld—and its most famous resident, Shamu the killer whale—*are* San Diego. You could easily spend a day exploring the park. Highlights include Shamu's water show (sit up front if you want to get splashed), the Penguin Encounter, the Manatee Rescue, and a new thrill ride called Shipwreck Rapids. This is a day's excursion where the two of you can while away the hours. Shamu the killer whale performs daily, and the penguin pen is a hoot. For a really touching encounter, sign up for the **Dolphin Interaction Program** (800–380–3202; $135 per person). You'll learn about bottlenose dolphins, then don a wetsuit to wade into the pool to meet a dolphin in person. This is a very popular program, so you'll need to book some months in advance.

FOR MORE ROMANCE

If you can't get enough of San Diego's colorful beach culture, check out the nearby community of Ocean Beach. This neighborhood is home to an intriguing mix of aging 1960s hippies and teen surfers, who frequent the tattoo and body-piercing shops. If getting your sweetheart's name engraved on your biceps is going a bit too far, you can always browse through the antiques stores and secondhand record shops that line Newport Avenue. Don't miss lunch at **South Beach Bar & Grill** (5059 Newport Avenue; 619-226-4577; inexpensive). If you haven't tried San Diego's culinary contribution—the fish taco—this is the place to go. The extensive menu features seafood tacos, burritos and quesadillas prepared to order. The lobster tacos are pure heaven.

A Whale-Watching Adventure

DANA POINT

IDWAY BETWEEN SAN DIEGO AND LOS ANGELES is Dana Point, a little jewel of a harbor that's one of the loveliest in Southern California. The community has a seafaring tradition that dates back to the early 1800s, when New England sailors came to trade with the mission in nearby San Juan Capistrano. Today you'll find mostly pleasure craft docked in the harbor's large marina. This itinerary places you in a cozy clifftop inn or a lavish resort, with plenty of time to explore by bicycle and glimpse the migrating California gray whales on your own seafaring excursion.

PRACTICAL NOTES: It may be sunny and warm on the shore, but the breeze really picks up out on the water. Don't forget warm jackets, sunglasses, and sunscreen. Hot drinks will probably be served onboard ship, but it's nice to have your own Thermos of hot chocolate or gourmet coffee. It's also smart to bring a pair of binoculars. Whale-watching season technically runs from December to early April, but for the best chance of seeing the whales, schedule your trip in late February or March. These majestic mammals are returning to Alaska during that period and tend to swim closer to shore. Combine this with Itinerary 25 to nearby San Juan Capistrano to see the old Spanish mission that attracted New England traders.

DAY ONE: *Morning*

Dana Point is an easy, one-hour drive up the coast from San Diego. To avoid morning rush hour traffic, have a relaxing breakfast at home, then depart midmorning. Follow Interstate 5 north, then take the Beach Cities exit to Pacific Coast Highway. This lands you in Dana Point.

This small, upscale town is a bit of anomaly in Southern California. Where you typically find evidence of the area's Spanish-Colonial and Mexican roots, Dana Point has a distinctly New England flair. That's because it was discovered by author-seaman Richard Henry Dana, who came from Boston in 1835 as a young man aboard the trading brig *Pilgrim*. He later chronicled his adventures in *Two Years Before the Mast*.

Your room may not be ready yet, so deposit your bags at the **Blue Lantern Inn** (34343 Street of the Blue Lantern; 949–661–1304 or 800–950–1236; $150–$210, including breakfast and afternoon tea). This twenty-nine-room gem was tailor-made for romantic getaways— each room has a four-poster bed, a fireplace, and an oversize bathroom with a roomy spa tub. The inn sits high atop a bluff overlooking Dana Point Harbor, and the tower rooms are the most requested. They have 180-degree ocean and harbor views with private patios or balconies, and the management leaves a bottle of chilled champagne in the room. One-night "Gourmet Getaway" packages, including dinner at a local restaurant, a Four Sisters Inns cookbook, and gourmet coffee beans with mugs, start at $170 and are available midweek.

If you crave the highest luxury, reserve a room at the **Ritz-Carlton, Laguna Niguel** (1 Ritz-Carlton Drive; 949–240–2000 or 800–241–3333; $285–$375). This 393-room, full-service resort also occupies a bluff with sweeping ocean views. Where the Blue Lantern Inn has the feel of a cozy New England B&B, the

Romance AT A GLANCE

* Stay at the small but luxurious **Blue Lantern Inn** (34343 Street of the Blue Lantern; 949–661–1304 or 800–950–1236) or the full-service **Ritz-Carlton, Laguna Niguel** (1 Ritz-Carlton Drive; 949–240–2000 or 800–241–3333). Both afford great views of the water.

* Borrow a bike or explore the blufftop trails by foot. Dana Point is one of the best whale-spotting locations in California, so keep an eye on the water. You could spot a group of whales blowing water out their spouts.

* Have dinner overlooking the water at the **Chart House** (34442 Street of the Green Lantern; 949–493–1183).

* Spend the morning on the water searching for California gray whales on their round-trip migration from Alaska to Baja California. Several local firms offer sightseeing tours. Contact the Orange County Marine Institute (24200 Dana Point Harbor Drive; 949–496–2274).

Ritz-Carlton is more like a grand Mediterranean palazzo. You'll find the spectacular flower arrangements and sumptuous European antiques that are the hallmark of any Ritz-Carlton, but the huge arched windows that open to the endless Pacific are the real draw. From December through March, the resort offers a "Whale-Watching Package," starting at $245 per night (with a two-night minimum on weekends), including accommodations, continental breakfast, a whale-watching excursion from Dana Point Harbor, and valet parking.

If you're staying at Blue Lantern Inn, request a picnic lunch ($20 for two), then borrow a couple of mountain bikes to spend the afternoon exploring the area.

DAY ONE: *Afternoon*

Pedal along the residential streets from the inn toward a series of well-manicured blufftop parks and trails, where you'll find plenty of inviting picnic spots and maybe spot a whale or two in the sea. At the end of the Street of the Amber Lantern, you'll find **Bluff Top Trail**. This trail is short (only a quarter-mile long), so lock up the bikes and walk. The path meanders over a wooden bridge, past a cluster of picturesque clifftop condominiums to *The Hide Drougher*, a striking sculpture commemorating the New England sailors who tossed cowhides from the cliffs to their ships in the cove below. The hides were traded by the residents of the mission in nearby San Juan Capistrano for finished shoes brought by ship from Boston factories. In fact peering down to the harbor below, you'll see a replica of Dana's ship, the *Pilgrim*.

Reclaim your wheels and continue pedaling south through the clifftop Heritage and Lantern Bay parks. In fact you can wind all the way through Lantern Bay Park to Doheny State Beach. Remember, though, you'll have to cycle up a fairly steep hill to the top of the bluff.

After all that pedaling you've certainly earned late-afternoon tea, wine and hors d'oeuvres at Blue Lantern Inn. Sit by the fire in the cozy lobby, surrounded by the owner's impressive collection of teddy bears, and peruse menus for local restaurants, or take your goodies out to the patio to watch the sunset. The Ritz-Carlton's Afternoon Tea ($25–$42; reservations recommended), served in The Library, is a traditional, high-brow repast of English tea, currant scones with Devonshire cream, cucumber sandwiches, and Scottish shortbread. Since this qualifies as more than an end-of-day snack, you may want to make it an early dinner.

Dana's Beloved Waters

Richard Henry Dana, author of Two Years Before the Mast, offers this observation: "San Juan is the only romantic spot in California. The country here for several miles is high table-land, running boldly to the shore, and breaking off in a steep hill, at the foot of which the waters of the Pacific are constantly dashing. For several miles the water washes the very bases of the hill, or breaks upon ledges and fragments of rocks which run out into the sea. Just where we landed was a small cove, or 'bight,' which gave us, at high tide, a few square feet of sand-beach between the sea and the bottom of the hill. This was the only landing-place. Directly above us, rose the perpendicular height of four or five hundred feet."

DAY ONE: *Evening*

DINNER

You'll find plenty of good restaurants in the area, but **Chart House** (34442 Street of the Green Lantern; 949-493-1183; expensive) has one of the best views in town. Perched on the cliffs just around the corner from Blue Lantern Inn, and a short drive from the Ritz-Carlton, it's a nice vantage point from which to see the twinkling lights in the harbor below. Wait a little longer for a window table, if you must—that great view is really why you're here. The menu is a mix of seafood, prime rib, and steaks. If you want, continue the weekend's New England theme with an order of clam chowder and a whole New England lobster.

After dinner return to the inn, where the staff has turned down the bed with a whimsical touch—the room's teddy bear resident has been turned on his head so a pair of gourmet chocolates can be balanced on his paws. Maybe draw a bath in the whirlpool tub, light the fireplace, and settle in to watch *An Affair to Remember*, *The Way We Were*, and other romantic flicks on the in-room video player.

DAY TWO: *Morning*

BREAKFAST

The breakfast buffet at Blue Lantern Inn is serious business—a smorgasbord of hot oatmeal, fresh-baked breads and pastries, a breakfast quiche, bagels,

and fruit. If the weather is fine, dine at a table on the patio and read the morning paper the management thoughtfully left by your door. Breakfast at the inn is included in the room rate, but for $5.00 per person, you can have breakfast served in bed. Staying at the Ritz-Carlton, Laguna Niguel? Order breakfast from room service, or head to the casual Terrace Restaurant.

California gray whales make an annual, 12,000-mile, round-trip trek from Alaska's chilly Bering Sea to the warm waters of Baja California. Since they stay fairly close to shore, to elude predators, you may spot them from the shore. **Lookout Park**, next to the Blue Lantern Inn, is a good vantage point from which to scan the sea. Another option is to join a morning whale-watching cruise. **Dana Wharf Sport Fishing** (34675 Street of the Golden Lantern; 949–496–5794) is the biggest whale-watching tour operator in the harbor. Trips depart at 10:00 A.M., noon, and 2:00 P.M. daily during the December-April season. Two-hour tours are $14 per person. For a trip with a more educational bent, the **Orange County Marine Institute** (24200 Dana Point Harbor Drive; 949–496–2274) offers two-and-a-half-hour tours on Saturdays and Sundays aboard the research vessel *Sea Explorer* for $20 per person. You'll learn how scientists track the whales' movement. You'll also investigate sea life in onboard touch tanks and have the chance to examine the plankton that make up a whale's diet when the researchers do a "mud grab" to gather materials from the ocean floor.

Unlike friendly dolphins, whales aren't likely to swim right up to the boat. If you spot a plume of vaporized water shooting up to 12 feet into the air, that's the sign of whale surfacing to breathe. More should follow, because whales travel in packs of two to six. If you're really lucky, you'll see a whale "spyhopping"—poking its head out of the water. If you see one of these 50-foot beasts "breach"—leap out of the water to splash on its back or side—it's a rare thrill indeed.

DAY TWO: *Afternoon*

LUNCH

The sea air encourages a hearty appetite. Casual and reliably good, the **Harbor Grill** (Mariner's Village, 34499 Street of the Golden Lantern, 949–240–1416; moderate) is a local favorite. Wait for a patio table so you can enjoy the sunshine and watch the passersby on the harborfront. Order a plate of fish and chips, or try the grilled shrimp with cilantro and green chili salsa for a more Southwestern flavor.

Walk off lunch with a stroll through Mariner's Village, a waterfront complex of yacht brokers and shops. A new boat may not be on your shopping list, but you can surprise her with lingerie from **Millefleurs** (34495 Street of the Golden Lantern; 949–248–7668) or a pretty bauble from the **Murata Pearl Company** (34511 Street of the Golden Lantern; 949–496–3332). Or stroll along **Doheny State Beach**, just south of the harbor (parking is $5.00 per vehicle), before heading home.

FOR MORE ROMANCE

Ready to pop the question? You don't have to be a guest to take advantage of The Ritz-Carlton, Laguna Niguel's "Proposal Package." For $250 the management sets the stage for a romantic betrothal: an overstuffed chair for the lady, a pillow for her suitor to kneel on, a table set with linen and silver, a bucket of chilled champagne, and fragrant rose petals strewn about the area. Choose from a variety of locations—the Gazebo, the Sunset Terrace, a secluded garden, or even the beach. It's unlikely anyone can refuse a proposal this romantic.

SAN DIEGO SKYLINE

Urban Affairs

Heart of the City

CLASSIC SAN DIEGO

THE BEAUTY OF SAN DIEGO'S HISTORIC GASLAMP QUARTER is that it brings together all the best elements of the city's revitalized downtown area. You have the charm of restored Victorian-era buildings, hopping nightlife, and first-rate shopping at pedestrian-friendly Horton Plaza—all displayed against the nautical backdrop of San Diego Bay. Wander hand in hand through the quarter, or see the sights while snuggled together in the back of a pedicab or horse-drawn carriage. This long weekend itinerary allows you to enjoy San Diego's casual ambience by day, then dress up a little to step out on the town by night.

PRACTICAL NOTES: San Diego's compact downtown waterfront district is easy to see by foot. Even better, its central location means you don't really need a car to explore other areas. You can catch the trolley from the station on the corner of India and C streets to ride all the way south to the Mexican border, or take a short ride north to Old Town. The Santa Fe Train Depot is on Kettner Boulevard if you want to catch the train to the North County communities of Solana Beach and Carlsbad. Or hop on the ferry and cross the bay to Coronado. Check out the itineraries for Coronado (Itinerary 1), Carlsbad (Itinerary 4), Old Town (Itinerary 9) and Tijuana (Itinerary 20) for ideas.

DAY ONE: *Morning*

Downtown and the waterfront are chockablock with hotels, but the historic **Horton Grand Hotel** (311 Island Avenue; 619–544–1886 or 800–542–1886; $119–$189) boasts nostalgic, Victorian whimsy. This 108-room gem in the

heart of the Gaslamp Quarter has quite a past. It's actually two structures that were scheduled for demolition in the 1970s but were rescued and married on this spot. One was a hotel, the other was a boardinghouse where, in the 1880s, former OK Corral gunslinger Wyatt Earp lived for a spell. The whole genteel affair sits on the site of a former bordello, and the hotel's dining room is named for its madam, Ida Bailey. No two rooms are decorated alike, although they all have cozy gas fireplaces, antiques, and lace curtains, completing the air of Victorian authenticity (but as a nod to modern needs, rooms have microwaves, hair dryers and other amenities). If you wind up in room 309, the hotel's resident ghost, the late Roger Whitacker, will be your roommate.

Another option is the **Westgate Hotel** (1055 Second Avenue; 619–238–1818 or 800–221–3802; $219–$269). Decorated with French antiques, grand chandeliers, and gilt-framed mirrors, the Westgate is a touch of Versailles in San Diego. Its European formality isn't for everyone, but the guest rooms are among the largest in the city, and their floor-to-ceiling windows afford terrific views of the bay or the mountains of East County.

Romance
AT A GLANCE

* Stay at the **Horton Grand Hotel** (311 Island Avenue; 619–544–1886 or 800–542–1886), a Victorian-era treasure in the heart of the Gaslamp Quarter. Or opt for the formal European elegance of the **Westgate Hotel** (1055 Second Avenue; 619–238–1818 or 800–221–3802).

* Explore the **Star of India**, a restored, nineteenth-century tall-masted ship docked in San Diego Bay. This majestic vessel is part of the **Maritime Museum** (1306 North Harbor Drive; 619–234–9153).

* Enjoy lunch on the water at the **Fish Market** (750 North Harbor Drive; 619–232–3474). If you need to jump-start your romantic spark, have a bite at the Oyster Bar.

* Have an early supper at **Croce's Restaurant & Jazz Bar** (802 Fifth Avenue; 619–233–4355), then catch a performance at one of the neighborhood's many theaters.

* Explore the stores in the inviting **Horton Plaza** (corner of Broadway and First; 619–238–1596) and check out the local art scene at the many small galleries in the Gaslamp Quarter.

* Dance under the stars on a twilight dinner cruise with **San Diego Harbor Excursions** (619–234–4111) aboard the Victorian sternwheeler MV Monterey.

* Snuggle up for a moonlight horse-drawn carriage ride along the waterfront with **Cinderella Carriage Company** (619–239–8080).

Fly Boy,

Fly Me to the Moon

Kansas City Barbecue (610 West Market Street, 619–231–9680; inexpensive) looks like any other low-rent barbecue joint by the railroad tracks. But look closely, and you'll recognize it as the spot where Tom Cruise crooned "You've Lost That Lovin' Feeling" to Kelly McGillis in the film Top Gun. *That movie—a romantic postcard to the heroes of the now-defunct U.S. Navy Top Gun fighter-pilot school in Miramar—was filmed in and around San Diego. Tom also cruised his motorcycle up the steep Laurel Street hill with the airport, bay, and setting sun in the background.*

Depending on availability, you can reserve the Sweet Getaway package. Priced at $175 a night, it comes with accommodations, a bottle of champagne, and a box of chocolates—not a bad start to your romantic weekend.

What better place to start a San Diego trip than by the water? After checking into your hotel, take a walk along the harbor—a real treat when it's a clear, blustery day. From the foot of Ash Street, you'll see that the boats in the harbor are a vivid reminder that San Diego has a rich maritime history. Vessels range from pleasure craft to cruise ships to U.S. Navy aircraft carriers (after all, San Diego is a navy town). Nowhere is the romance of the sea more apparent than in the *Star of India*, a lovingly restored nineteenth century tall-masted merchant ship. This beauty sailed around the world (21 times!) before it docked in San Diego Bay in 1926. The ship is part of the floating **Maritime Museum** (1306 North Harbor Drive; 619–234–9153; admission $5.00), headquartered aboard the nineteenth century ferry vessel the *Berkeley* (which has a permanent collection of props from the film *Titanic*).

DAY ONE: *Afternoon*

LUNCH

Continue south along the water to Tuna Harbor, named for San Diego's once thriving tuna fishing industry. It's a fitting location for the bustling

Fish Market (750 North Harbor Drive; 619–232–3474; moderate to expensive) restaurant, where you have several dining options. Grab a quick bite at the oyster or sushi bar, or wait for a waterside table at the moderately priced downstairs restaurant, from which you can watch boats drift by on the glittering bay. If you want a more upscale experience, head upstairs to the pricier **Top of the Market**. Upstairs or down, you can select from an ample menu of fresh local and imported seafood. Start with the tiger prawn cocktail or, for a south of the border taste, the fresh scallop ceviche tostada. The fresh catch of the day, typically salmon, red snapper, John Dory, monkfish, or catfish, can be ordered broiled, grilled, fried, or Cajun-style.

A short walk south brings you to **Seaport Village**, a popular restaurant and shopping complex. Browse through gift shops and galleries; if you feel playful, share a pony ride with your beloved on the circa-1890 Broadway Flying Horse Carousel. Make a stop at the **Soap Opera** (619–230–1300), where you can pick up a few bars of Sea*Coast Soapworks' locally made soap that pays homage to San Diego's surf culture. Pick up a bar of Windansea Tangerine or Chocolate Wave.

DAY ONE: *Evening*

DINNER

You're going to the theater tonight, so grab an early, light dinner in the Gaslamp Quarter. Lively bistros and cafes line the streets, and you can't go wrong with any of them. Watch the world go by from a sidewalk table at **Croce's Restaurant & Jazz Bar** (802 Fifth Avenue; 619–233–4355; moderate), a lively eatery and bar run by singer Jim Croce's widow, Ingrid. She's also the proprietor of the adjacent **Croce's Top Hat Bar & Grill**, a good spot for late-night entertainment.

There is lots of live theater in downtown. In the heart of the Gaslamp Quarter is the **Horton Grand Theatre** (444 Fourth Avenue; 619–234–9583). At press time the comedy hit *Triple Espresso: A Highly Caffeinated Comedy* was in its second year. The **Civic Theater** (Third Avenue and B Street; 619–236–6510) usually hosts road shows of Broadway productions, while the **Sledgehammer Theatre** (St. Cecilia's Church, 1620 Sixth Avenue; 619– 544–1484) features cutting-edge works. The **San Diego Repertory Theater** (Lyceum Stage, 79 Horton Plaza; 619–235–8025) stages revivals and premieres new works. For great deals

on theater tickets, pop by the **Arts Tix** booth (28 Horton Plaza; 619-497-5000) in front of Horton Plaza.

The Gaslamp Quarter hops with bars and coffeehouses for an after-theater nightcap or cappuccino. Tucked away on F Street between Fourth and Fifth Avenues is **Café Lulu** (419 F Street; 619-238-0114; inexpensive), where decadent desserts, coffee drinks, and wine are served in a chic, Euro-minimalist setting.

DAY TWO: *Morning*

BREAKFAST

It takes awhile for the Gaslamp Quarter to wake up in the morning, so take advantage of your hotel's hospitality and enjoy a leisurely and romantic breakfast served in your room.

Midmorning, amble over to **Horton Plaza** (corner of Broadway and First; 619-238-1596). Built in the 1980s, this open-air, multilevel mall is an architectural oddity in the midst of the neighborhood's Victoriana. It looks like an Italian Renaissance marketplace on acid—lots of arches, columns, and fountains done up in a colorful Crayola palette. For many, it's the heart of downtown. And the shopping isn't bad, either. You'll find Nordstrom, Banana Republic, and the usual mall suspects.

DAY TWO: *Afternoon*

LUNCH

Horton Plaza has plenty of eateries, from fast-food outlets to sit-down restaurants, but walk a few blocks into the Gaslamp Quarter and you'll find **Trattoria Mama Anna** (644 Fifth Avenue; 619-235-8144; moderate), an unpretentious, family-run Italian restaurant. Their wonderful fresh-baked breads are a delight, and their focaccia sandwiches are plenty for two to share. On a fine day, sit at a sidewalk table and watch the world go by.

Aside from shops, downtown San Diego is also known for art galleries. More than twenty of them are packed into the area, and downtown lofts are home to many local artists. At the end of April there is the annual Sony Artwalk (619-615-1090), during which artists open their studios to the public. Some

local galleries to check out include the Mexican-themed **Galeria Dos Damas** (415 Market Street; 619–231–3030), **A Level Above** (eighth floor at the Clarion Hotel Bay View, 660 K Street; 619–696–0234), and the **Soma Gallery** (343 Fourth Avenue; 619–232–3955), best known for contemporary art.

For a macabre eye-opener, take a peek into the **Museum of Death** (548 Fifth Avenue; 619–338–8153; admission $5.00). This tiny, basement-level museum has a hair-raising display of shrunken heads, coffins, mortician's tools, and artifacts *d'morte*. If that proves a bone-chilling experience, pop next door to warm up with a wee dram at **The Field** (544 Fifth Avenue; 619–232–9840), an Irish pub.

DAY TWO: *Evening*

DINNER

Put on your dancing shoes for a twilight dinner cruise on the bay with **San Diego Harbor Excursions** (619–234–4111; $50–$69 per person). Rendezvous at the Broadway Pier (where Broadway runs into the bay), where you'll board the *Spirit of San Diego*, a newly remodeled, trilevel yacht with an open-air observation deck, cocktail bars, dance floors, and a lounge, or the MV *Monterey*, a Victorian stern-wheeler. On either boat you'll be taken on a two-and-a-half-hour cruise around the bay, taking in views of the city skyline, Coronado, and the San Diego–Coronado Bay Bridge. But be prompt—the boats depart at 7:00 P.M. sharp!

Afterward, stroll down to the Harbor House restaurant at Seaport Village to take a ride in one of **Cinderella Carriage Company's**

Gaslamp Gingerbread

While roaming around the Gaslamp Quarter, don't forget to look up. Otherwise, you might miss the lavish confectionery of the neighborhood's Victorian-era buildings. With intricate plasterwork, lacy wrought-iron railings, and vibrant rainbow colors, "they are perfect symbols of an era which was not given to understatement," John Mass remarked in his book The Gingerbread Age. Tony boutiques and chichi restaurants may occupy these gentrified buildings today, but it's not hard to imagine the Gaslamp's racy, red-light past. Why, Wyatt Earp blew into town in 1887 and went into business as a gambling saloon proprietor. If you want to learn more about the district, join a docent-led walking tour. They depart every Saturday at 11:00 a.m. from the William Heath Davis House (corner of Fourth and Island Avenues). Tours cost $5.00 per person; call 619–233–4692 for more information.

(619–239–8080) white, Amish-built, horse-drawn buggies. On a clear night, with a blanket draped over your legs and two glasses of champagne in your hands, it's perhaps the most romantic way to see the waterfront. Tours range from fifteen minutes to an hour at rates of $25 to $80.

DAY THREE: *Morning*

Watch the boats in the harbor while you enjoy a morning walk or jog along the waterfront. You can follow the footpath all the way around the tip of the Embarcadero and cut back through Seaport Village.

BREAKFAST

Wrap up your downtown weekend with a flourish over Sunday champagne brunch at the Westgate Hotel's **Le Fountainebleau Restaurant** (619–557–3655; $29.95 per person; reservations recommended). Cruise the buffet, where chefs prepare made-to-order omelettes and crepes, as well as pasta, pâté and caviar. Leave room for some of the tempting little pastries.

FOR MORE ROMANCE

Just north of downtown, San Diego's **Little Italy** stretches for several blocks along India Street. This neighborhood is indeed petite compared to the Italian boroughs in other large cities, but it's a vibrant enclave of terrific restaurants (Italiano, of course) and shops. We recommend the gelato made on the premises at **Cafe Zucchero** (1731 India Street; 619–531–1731; moderate). You may want to have dinner there first, since the cafe's fresh pasta and and wood-fired pizzas are winners (try the Gamberi pizza smothered in pesto, mozzarella, and fresh shrimp). Request a table on the back patio. With charming frescoes painted on the walls and intimate, candlelit tables, it's one of San Diego's best-kept romantic secrets. Also stroll through the imported treasures at **India Street Antiques** (2360 India Street; 619–231–3004).

Eden in the City

BALBOA PARK

DJACENT TO DOWNTOWN IS ONE OF SAN DIEGO'S most romantic spots. Much-beloved Balboa Park wraps up tranquil gardens, historic buildings, theaters, and fourteen museums in one tidy 1,200-acre package. This sanctuary offers all the ingredients for a full day of romance, followed by a great date night at the theater.

The park was built for the 1915-1916 Panama-California Exposition, then greatly expanded as a Depression-era public works project for the 1935 World Expo. Because of the theme of the expo, the architecture is solidly Spanish-Colonial Revival—lots of elaborate plasterwork and redolent with old-world charm that's a surprising find in such a young city. Once you've check out the museums and meandered through the gardens, you'll see why Balboa Park is a favorite venue with local courting couples, as well as a popular wedding spot.

PRACTICAL NOTES: In general the park is quieter on weekdays. Many museums are closed on Mondays, and a number waive admission fees on one or two Tuesdays a month. Though weekends are busier, you'll still find plenty of activity with buskers, vendors, and even palm readers setting up shop along El Prado. If visiting museums and galleries is high on your agenda, stop by the **Balboa Park Visitors Information Center** (619–239–1100) in the House of Hospitality to purchase a pair of Passports to Balboa Park ($21 each). They cover admission to twelve of the park's museums, and they're valid for a week so you don't have to see everything in one day. Don't forget to wear comfortable walking shoes, since this is a place to be explored on foot. Since you're staying overnight at the Balboa Park Inn, it's easy to add a day at the San Diego Zoo (Itinerary 12).

Romance
AT A GLANCE

* Check out the anthropological exhibits at the **San Diego Museum of Man** (1350 El Prado; 619–239–2001) and enjoy a local treat—a fresh, handmade corn tortilla.

* Visit the European Masters at the small but delightful **Timken Museum** (1500 El Prado; 619–239–5548) or catch a traveling exhibition at the **San Diego Museum of Art** (1450 El Prado; 619–232–7931).

* Have lunch amid the Rodins, Calders, and Mirós at the San Diego Museum of Art's **Sculpture Garden Cafe & Bistro** (1450 El Prado; 619–696–1990).

* Explore the cool, shady recesses of the **Botanical Building,** the two-acre **Palm Canyon,** and the recently restored **Alcazar Garden.**

* Be serenaded by a free concert at the **Spreckels Organ Pavilion** in the park.

* Check into the **Balboa Park Inn** (3402 Park Boulevard; 619–298–0823 or 800–938–8181), where a whirlpool tub and a wide range of room themes make this a relaxing spot after a full day on your feet in the park.

* Have a bite of pretheater dinner at **Laurel** (505 Laurel Street; 619–239–2222) or **Mister A's** (2550 Fifth Avenue, Number 111; 619–239–1377), then take in a performance at the **Old Globe Theatre** (1363 Old Globe Way; 619–239–2255).

DAY ONE: *Morning*

Plan to arrive at the park around midmorning, once the museums and other attractions have opened. Enter from the park's west side, over the picturesque Cabrillo Bridge—the only cantilevered bridge in the state. Crossing the bridge you'll be treated to the spectacular downtown skyline view, and the impossibly low-flying commercial airplanes as they approach San Diego's Lindbergh Field.

Walking in under the archway at the **San Diego Museum of Man** (1350 El Prado, 619–239–2001; $4.00 per person) you'll pass through the Spanish-style California Quadrangle. During the day the courtyard is usually filled with vendors selling colorful cultural gifts. The museum's stately bell tower will look familiar to film buffs. Orson Welles borrowed it as the setting for Xanadu in *Citizen Kane*. The museum is a favorite with kids of all ages, who relish the anthropological exhibits—Mayan artifacts, Egyptian mummies, and the like. A special treat, however, are the handmade corn tortillas drenched in butter (50 cents each), available inside the museum.

Continue down El Prado, the main thoroughfare in the park, and you'll pass most of the park's museums. The **Mingei International Museum of Art** (1439 El Prado; 619–239–0003; $5.00 per person) houses a terrific collection of pottery, textiles, jewelry, dolls, and other artifacts from around the world. Just across the main plaza is the **San Diego Museum of Art**

(1450 El Prado; 619–232–7931; $7.00 per person), which features a permanent collection of Dutch, Italian, and Spanish Baroque masterworks, as well as ancient Asian treasures. The museum also also headlines several major touring exhibitions each year (with separate admission). If a major exhibit is at the museum, you'll need to purchase tickets well in advance.

Next to the Museum of Art is the **Timken Museum** (1500 El Prado; 619–239–5548) with its free collection of paintings by the European Masters, early American works, and Russian icons. Continuing east along El Prado, you'll come to the **Museum of Photographic Arts** (1649 El Prado; 619–238–7559; $3.50 per person), which features an ever-changing exhibit schedule.

Just past the Timken is one of the city's signature sights—a long lily pond that reflects the striking wood-lath **Botanical Building**. Even on the warmest days, this open-frame structure offers a cool retreat for more than 2,100 exotic tropical plants, as well as visitors.

DAY ONE: *Afternoon*

LUNCH

Ready for a spot of lunch? Your options range from convenient hot dog stands located throughout the park to the San Diego Museum of Art's **Sculpture Garden Cafe & Bistro** (1450 El Prado; 619–696–1990; moderate), where you can relax among the handiwork of Rodin, Calder, and Miró.

If it's a Sunday afternoon, don't miss the free, hour-long concert at the **Spreckels Organ Pavilion**. These kick off every week at 2:00 P.M. The 4,400-pipe organ has been the park's pride and joy since the Panama–California Exposition.

After lunch it's time for a romantic stroll through the park's lush, colorful gardens. One of the most unusual is the **Japanese Friendship Garden** (open Tuesdays, Fridays, Saturdays, and Sundays, 10:00 A.M. to 4:00 P.M.), located just in front of Spreckels Organ Pavilion. The garden has recently completed a major expansion and renovation that includes a new teahouse and koi pond. You'll also find a traditional Japanese sand and stone garden, and a wisteria arbor viewing area that overlooks the canyon below.

Across from the Japanese Garden is two-acre **Palm Canyon,** where wooden bridges and walkways wind through 450 towering tropical palms. And you don't have to be green thumbs to appreciate the **Alcazar Garden,** located behind the **House of Charm** (1439 El Prado). Patterned after the

gardens of Alcazar Castle in Seville, Spain, this small, formal garden features some 7,000 annuals for a vivid, year-round display of color, as well as ornate fountains and brightly colored Moorish tiles. With its protective wall of boxwood hedges, the garden is a secluded spot in the park—a perfect retreat for a twosome seeking a little peace and quiet.

 Now is a good time to check into your room at the **Balboa Park Inn** (3402 Park Boulevard; 619–298–0823 or 800–938–8181; $85–$200). Housed in a series of pink-adobe Mission-style buildings on the edge of the park, the inn has twenty-six rooms and suites. Ask for detailed descriptions when making reservations, since all the rooms are different. Your options range from the Caribbean-theme Aruba room, which boasts a whirlpool tub, to over-the-top Tara Suite, with its canopy bed and marble-mantle fireplace. One of the best bets is the Las Palomas suite. It has a large private balcony overlooking the park.

DAY ONE: *Evening*

DINNER

The park is lovely during the day, but it's also lively at night. Begin with pretheater dinner at **Laurel** (505 Laurel Street, 619–239–2222; expensive), which features French cuisine with a Mediterranean influence. If you're in the mood to dress up and want to step into an authentic martini-era hangout, **Mister A's Restaurant** (2550 Fifth Avenue, Number 111; 619–239–1377; expensive) is the place. The waiters wear black tie, and jackets are a must for male diners. Once *the* fine-dining spot for San Diego's movers and shakers, Mister A's retro ambience is helping it stage a comeback. At sunset the panoramic view of the city bathed in a golden glow is pretty spectacular, too.

Finish the evening with a performance at the **Simon Edison Center for the Performing Arts** (619–239–2255; tickets from $34). This complex houses three theaters, the centerpiece being the **Old Globe Theatre,** a replica of the famed theater where Shakespeare performed in London (1362 Old Globe Way, 619–239–2255; tickets from $34). You'll also find the intimate **Cassius Carter Centre Stage** and, in summer, you can enjoy Shakespeare under the stars at the outdoor **Lowell Davies Festival Theater.** The Old Globe has a renowned repertory company and features major productions of classics and new works. Major stars, such as Alan Alda, John Goodman, Bebe Neuwirth, Victor Garber, and Campbell Scott, among others, have trod the boards here.

If you believe chocolate is the food of love, plan a trip to **Extraordinary Desserts** (2929 Fifth Avenue; 619–293–7001; inexpensive). It's a short drive from the theater and definitely worth the effort. Chef-owner Karen Krasne specializes in one thing: sweet nirvana. Line up with the local sugar junkies to peruse her selection of lavish cakes, creative cookies, muffins, tarts, and other sinful delights. Even seemingly simple items are given the gourmet treatment. If you're not hungry for a slice of flower-topped chocolate torte sprinkled with edible gold dust, a fresh chocolate chip cherry cookie will satisfy your sweet tooth. Linger over your goodies in a cozy, candlelit booth or at a patio table.

DAY TWO: *Morning*

BREAKFAST

The park is a popular spot with walkers and joggers, and there are plenty of trails threading through the trees. If that's more than you want to take on this morning, sleep in, then linger over the continental breakfast the innkeepers deliver to your room.

From the inn it's a pleasant walk along Park Boulevard to the park's east entrance. One thing that's sure to catch your eye is the **Balboa Park Carousel**, which dates back to 1910. Pay $1.25 and take a whirl with your sweetheart on one of the original, hand-carved ponies. Continuing into the park you'll come upon the **Spanish Village Art Center** (1770 Village Drive; 619–233–9050). True to its name this enclave is modeled after a sleepy Spanish village and is home to forty-one art studios. You'll find everything from glass-bead jewelry to paintings and sculptures. After browsing and possibly buying, head to the **Reuben H. Fleet Space Theater and Science Center** (1875 El Prado; 619–238–1233; free), which has dozens of fun and educational interactive exhibits. Also find out what's playing in the center's OMNIMAX theater (the world's first) for an early matinee of an IMAX flick. Ticket prices vary, depending on what's showing.

FOR MORE ROMANCE

Want to learn more about Balboa Park? You have plenty of free tours to choose from. Hour-long Architectural Heritage Tours are offered once a month, as are walks led by the Balboa Birders. Volunteers with the San Diego Natural History Museum's **Canyoneers** (619–232–3821, ext.7) lead hikes through the park, as well as throughout the county on weekends

throughout the year except August. On Saturdays volunteer horticulturists lead one-hour walks, departing from the Botanical Building at 10:00 A.M. Contact the **Balboa Park Visitors Information Center** (619–239–1100) for details, or check out their web page at www.balboapark.org.

Where Love Begins
OLD TOWN

STROLLING MARIACHIS SERENADE WHILE YOU SIP MARGARITAS on a cool, bougainvillea-shaded patio. Afterward you retire to a superb B&B in a restored Victorian home. Experiences like these bring the romance of San Diego's Mexican-American heritage to life. Aptly named, Old Town is the historic heart of San Diego, a lively crossroads where the city's roots as an eighteenth century Spanish garrison meld with its more recent past as a thriving outpost of the new American state of California in the nineteenth century. Today visitors find a self-contained destination with galleries, shops, and festive eateries just steps from a terrific inn. This itinerary invites you to explore the city's past at your own pace.

PRACTICAL NOTES: Old Town is awash with locals and tourists for the annual Mexican Cinco de Mayo celebration (that's May 5, of course). If you decide to brave the crowds (there's plenty of live folkloric entertainment to make it worthwhile), expect long waits at local restaurants. The park also is festive during the first week of November, when you'll see whimsical and ghoulish altars commemorating the Mexican Día de los Muertos (Day of the Dead), as well as at Christmastime, when Mexican-style luminarias (sand-filled paper bags with candles) cast a gentle glow. Any time of year Old Town's proximity to the major freeways makes it a convenient base for longer stays in San Diego. You may choose to combine this trip with Classic San Diego (Itinerary 7). A San Diego Trolley stop in Old Town makes for an easy connection to downtown.

DAY ONE: *Morning*

Occupying a pair of lovingly restored Victorian houses in Heritage Park, **Heritage Park Inn** (2470 Heritage Park Row; 619–299–6832 or

Romance
AT A GLANCE

* Choose one of the twelve rooms at **Heritage Park Inn** (2470 Heritage Park Row; 619–299–6832 or 800–995–2470). Stays here include afternoon tea on the veranda and breakfast served by candlelight in the main dining room.

* Do a little shopping at **Bazaar del Mundo** (2754 Calhoun Street; 619–296–3161), where you can pick up terrific imported housewares, jewelry, and furniture at a series of boutiques surrounding a Mexican-style courtyard.

* Relax over margaritas and lunch at **Casa de Bandini Restaurant** (2754 Calhoun Street; 619–297–8211). Housed in a historic home, it's also one of the city's best-loved Mexican restaurants.

* Check out the historic sites of Old Town, including **La Casa de Estudillo** (Mason Street, between San Diego Avenue and Calhoun Street; 619–298–2482) and the haunted (so the docents promise) **Whaley House** (2482 San Diego Avenue; 619–298–2482).

* Time to choose an engagement ring? Take a look at the sparklers in the **Diamond Source** (2474 San Diego Avenue; 619–299–6900).

* Plan dinner at Old Town's finest, **Cafe Pacifica** (2414 San Diego Avenue; 619–291–6666).

* Spend a morning exploring the pretty residential streets and shops of the **Mission Hills neighborhood.** Your innkeepers will give you a detailed map with suggested walking routes. Then investigate the archaeological dig to unearth the remains of California's first Spanish mission at **Presidio Park.**

800–995–2470; $90–$225) is one of those doll-house-darling bed-and-breakfast places that gets it right. On a hill overlooking Old Town, this park is a picture-perfect enclave of Queen Anne and Italianate Victorian-era homes rescued and relocated from other parts of the city. The inn boasts a dozen rooms, each individually decorated. You'll find plenty of great touches—antique stained-glass windows, furnishings, clothes, and toys highlight the inn's Victorian theme, while comfy feather-beds and cozy robes spoil you. If you're celebrating a special occasion, be sure to mention it when making reservations. Owner Nancy Helsper is happy to help with romantic suggestions, from arranging in-room massages to securing priority reservations at local restaurants. For an additional $55, the innkeeper will put a plush teddy bear with a bouquet of roses and a box of gourmet chocolates in your room. But which room to request? The Turret, with a sitting room overlooking the park, is a popular spot for proposals. Couples who want to stay in should request one of the three rooms with whirlpool tubs for two.

It's just a short walk to the sights of Old Town, yet you can escape the crowds when you are ready to. Perhaps the heart of Old Town is the vibrant **Bazaar del Mundo** (2754 Calhoun Street; 619–296–3161). Built on the remains of an authentic Mexican casa, it's a lively and colorful complex of boutiques and restaurants situated around a central court-

yard where authentic mariachis play their festive brand of guitar and brass music. Start at one end and you can peruse the eighteen interconnected stores, picking up oddities as you go. Mixed in are stores for kitchen furnishings, Southwestern clothing, fabrics, furniture, books, cactus plants, and other knickknacks. Homebodies should investigate the kitchen accessories at **Design Center Accessories** (619-296-3161), as well as the folk art and crafts at **Artes de Mexico** (619-296-3266). **The Gallery** (619-296-3161) has a winning selection of surprisingly affordable Native American silver and turquoise jewelry for him and her. Not into shopping? Bazaar del Mundo features free entertainment—those ever-present mariachis and Mexican Ballet Folkorico dancers in traditional garb—on weekends.

DAY ONE: *Afternoon*

LUNCH

You're in Old Town, so naturally you should have Mexican fare. You'll see several eateries in Bazaar del Mundo, but we suggest you walk up the block to **Casa de Bandini Restaurant** (2754 Calhoun Street; 619-297-8211; moderate). This very popular Mexican restaurant is firmly rooted in the city's history. It occupies the former home of the Bandini family, which dates back to 1829. It was a grand home indeed, with its expansive balconies and porches designed to catch cool ocean breezes. Today the margaritas and *cervezas* flow freely, the tortilla chips and salsa are abundant, and the food is delicious. Wait for a patio table (you can lounge in the traditional Mexican leather chairs on the wide front porch while you wait). It's easy to fill up on the tortilla chips, so you may just want to share a quesadilla (cheese wrapped in a flour tortilla) and an order of *taquitos* (tasty rolled tacos) smothered in guacamole.

From Casa de Bandini continue your exploration of Old Town. The area is a six-block state park that preserves the city's early days in a series of restored historic buildings. Old Town looks like a Wild West movie set come to life—stores have wooden walkways and jutting wood beams. At any moment you expect Yul Brynner or Clint Eastwood to step out onto the streets, and you half expect the theme from *The Good, the Bad and the Ugly* to start up. Stop by the State Park Headquarters in the main square to pick up a map. One don't-miss spot is **La Casa de Estudillo** (Mason Street, right across from Casa de Bandini; 619-298-2482). Built in 1829 the house is a traditional Mexican adobe hacienda—a series of rooms that

open onto a central courtyard. You'll see the rooms furnished as they would have been in the nineteenth century. Also check out the blacksmith's shop at **Seeley Stables**, behind Casa de Bandini (Calhoun Street, between Twiggs and Mason Streets; 619–220–5427).

One of the great treats, however, is a visit to the **Whaley House** (2482 San Diego Avenue; 619–298–2482; admission $4.00 per person). Built in 1857 the four-bedroom, two-story house was the home of Thomas and Anna Whaley and their daughters until as late as 1953. But make sure to hold hands—the Whaley House is haunted. Docents share tales of Thomas Whaley's ghost wandering through the old courtroom in the house, waiting to be paid a debt owed to him by the city. Daughter Violet Whaley, who was mysteriously shot, haunts the premises, too, and an unidentified young girl is said to walk the halls at night.

Strolling along San Diego Avenue, the main road leading into Old Town, you'll see a somewhat touristy mix of T-shirt shops and souvenir vendors. But there are some interesting finds tucked among the tchotchkes. You'll find a number of shops selling Mexican-made pottery and ceramics. They're worth a stop, especially if you don't plan to head south of the border anytime soon. Pick up a bar of locally crafted, hard-milled soap, a scoop of fizzy bath salts, or other aromatic skin-care goodies at **U.S. Apothecary and Soap Shop** (2765 San Diego Avenue; 619–574–1115)—perfect for a predinner soak in your tub at the inn. Feeling extravagant? Take your honey to see the sparklers at the **Diamond Source** (2474 San Diego Avenue; 619–299–6900). Owners Carl Romaner and Marco Levy cut and set their diamond creations right on the premises of this glittering diamond store. It's similar to the famed diamond cutters of Amsterdam, Holland. You'll certainly find the perfect engagement ring there, as well as other dazzling trinkets.

By late afternoon you'll be ready to walk back to the inn and a refreshing respite. Afternoon tea is served at about 5:00 P.M. in the parlor or on the veranda. Tiered sandwich trays offer up a tempting selection of dainty finger sandwiches and fresh-baked cakes accompanied by an assortment of teas and lemonade.

DAY ONE: *Evening*

DINNER

Situated next to the tiny El Campo Santo Cemetery (final resting place of some of San Diego's earliest residents), you could say that **Cafe**

Pacifica (2414 San Diego Avenue; 619–291–6666; moderate to expensive) is in the "dead center" of town. While there is an endless choice of restaurants in Old Town, this is the best spot for an elegantly romantic repast. The menu emphasizes fresh seafood paired with locally grown herbs and vegetables (meat lovers will find good steak and lamb dishes, too). The presentation is always superlative, and a fine wine selection guarantees that the evening will have the perfect ending. Gentlemen, a jacket is certainly not out of place for this restaurant, although you needn't wear a tie.

Back at the inn you'll find your bed has been thoughtfully turned down with one of the resident teddy bears, a pair of chocolates, and aromatherapy "sweet dreams" pillows, and, for the lady, a rose.

DAY TWO: *Morning*

BREAKFAST

Breakfast is a romantic candlelit affair—complete with place cards—served in the inn's dining room. It's also a feast of choices, such as homemade granolas, baked Victorian French toast with apple cider syrup, poached pears in crème fraîche, eggs florentine, and country sausage. Enjoy, because you'll have ample opportunity to walk it off this morning.

After breakfast ask the innkeeper for a map of the neighborhood of Mission Hills, which sits on the hill just above the inn. This quiet but grand neighborhood is one of the oldest in the city, and it's a delightful blend of Craftsman, Spanish Colonial, Italianate, and Mission Revival homes. Grand estates rub shoulders with modest cottages, and you'll encounter small pockets of shops and restaurants, particularly along Goldfinch and West Lewis streets.

As you make your way back toward Old Town, stop for a cup of tea at the **Mission Hills Market Cafe** (1922-C Fort Stockton; 619–295–5353; inexpensive). Sit at one of the outdoor tables overlooking a canyon filled with eucalyptus trees. From there it's short walk down the hill to **Presidio Park,** site of California's first mission. Originally opened on this site in 1769, the mission was later moved inland to more fertile ground for livestock. The lovely white-adobe building you see today is a replica built in 1929, although nearby you can see an ongoing archaeological dig to uncover the mission's original foundations.

FOR MORE ROMANCE

Need a little lighthearted entertainment? *Forever Plaid* is the longest-running theatrical production in San Diego, and you can catch a performance at the **Theatre in Old Town** (4040 Twiggs Street; 619–688–2494; $23–$33). It's a ninety-minute musical comedy with a cast of four geeky guys singing their way through popular tunes of the 1950s and 1960s, including a very popular three-minute reenactment of the *Ed Sullivan Show*. Ask about the dinner theater packages at Cafe Pacifica.

Old Town has a convenient station for the San Diego Trolley. Hop on for a ride ($3.00 per person) to downtown, where you can explore the shops and restaurants of the lively Gaslamp Quarter. Check out Itinerary 7 for Classic San Diego for ideas.

Uptown Sweethearts

NEIGHBORHOOD DUET

VERY CITY HAS A TROVE OF GREAT NEIGHBORHOODS off the beaten tourist path, and San Diego is no exception. Just a short drive from downtown are two that, combined, make for a fun day of shopping and dining. Hillcrest may be the center of San Diego's gay community, but its lively streets, art house movie theaters, terrific shops, and some of the best restaurants in the city make it a popular date spot for couples of all persuasions. A short distance northeast of Hillcrest is the grand old residential neighborhood of Kensington, where you'll find antiques stores, funky secondhand clothing boutiques, a romantic dinner spot, and a revival movie house.

PRACTICAL NOTES: No need to start too bright and early. Plan a leisurely midmorning breakfast, and then let your day stretch into the evening. Parking is tight in these neighborhoods, especially in Hillcrest (where meter monitors keep close tabs on the time). It may be easier just to pay $5.00 and park in one of several lots. In Kensington, park on one of the residential streets just off Adams Avenue. If you want, you can combine this itinerary with Itinerary 8 to Balboa Park.

DAY ONE: *Morning*

BREAKFAST

Start with a midmorning nosh at favorite local spot, **Bread & Cie** (350 University Avenue; 619–683–9322; inexpensive). Modeled after the bakeries

Romance

AT A GLANCE

✻ Enjoy coffee and a nosh at **Bread & Cie** (350 University Avenue; 619- 683-9322), a spot locals favor to start their day with a slice of fresh-baked gourmet bread and steaming cup of joe.

✻ Spend a few hours browsing through the shops of Hillcrest. Pick up a pair of aromatherapy candles at **Cathedral** (435 University Avenue; 619–296–4046), or check out the TV-generation kitsch at **Babette Schwartz** (421 University Avenue; 619–220–7048).

✻ Share a light lunch and a carafe of the house red at **La Vache** (420 Robinson Avenue; 619–295–0214), a casual, country-style French bistro.

✻ Walk a mile south of La Vache to find one of the city's most romantic secret spots—the Spruce Street Suspension Footbridge.

✻ Pass the rest of the afternoon exploring the antiques shops and secondhand furniture, clothing, and new- and used-book stores along Adams Avenue, and then amble through the residential neighborhood of Kensington.

✻ Make reservations for dinner at the **Kensington Grill** (4055 Adams Avenue; 619–281–4014). If you arrive a little early, stop for a drink at the friendly bar and shoot some pool.

✻ Find out what's playing at the **Ken Cinema** (4061 Adams Avenue; 619–283–5909). Right next door to the Kensington Grill, this revival theater screens classic and cult films from around the world.

found in Cannes, France, Bread & Cie has a tempting selection of freshly baked breads. Flavors like garlic and goat cheese, anise fig, rosemary olive oil, and jalapeño cheese make for a tasty change of pace. Ask for samples before making your selection, and be sure to order a cappuccino to wash it down.

From Bread & Cie stroll along University and Fifth Avenues to check out the shops. Looking for just the right accessory for your house? **Column One** (401 University Avenue; 619–299–9074) has an affordable and eclectic selection of decorative house and garden items made from plaster molds—everything from Grecian urns to Egyptian cats to mirrors in Renaissance-style frames. On a completely different note, **Babette Schwartz** (421 University Avenue; 619–220–7048) offers a fun and kitschy collection of retro TV-generation cards, toys, and T-shirts. If you believe no romantic encounter is complete without flickering candles, stock up on fragrant aromatherapy candles and accessories (the wrought-iron candelabra will turn any bedroom into a setting suitable for a romance novel) at the moody and gothic **Cathedral** (435 University Avenue; 619–296–4046).

Book lovers can easily lose themselves among the stacks of the new- and used-book stores along Fifth Avenue. Two to check out are **Blue Door Literary Bookstore** (3823 Fifth Avenue; 619–298–8610), which specializes in new titles from small and alternative presses, and **Joseph Tabler Books** (3833 Fifth Avenue; 619–296–1424), which does a brisk business buying and selling used volumes. Tabler's art books are definitely worth investigating.

DAY ONE: *Afternoon*

LUNCH

One of the best deals in town is **La Vache** (420 Robinson Avenue; 619–295–0214; moderate), a casual, French-country bistro. The lunch menu features hearty soups, salads, sandwiches, cassoulet, and stews served at rough-hewn wood tables.

After such a delightful lunch, how about a lovely walk to one of San Diego's hidden romantic spots? Stroll a mile south of La Vache along Fourth Avenue to Spruce Street. Turn right, and 2 blocks west you'll come to the entrance of the **Spruce Street Suspension Footbridge**. This delightful, single-span bridge crosses Olive Park canyon, amid fragrant eucalyptus, pepper, and palm trees, with splendid views of downtown. The sturdy old wood-plank bridge actually sways as you stride across, so hold hands. If you're daring types, you might want to stop and smooch in the middle.

From Hillcrest, it's a five-minute drive to Adams Avenue, a long street that passes through North Park, Normal Heights, and Kensington. You'll find plenty of reasons to stop along Adams Avenue, which has a number of antiques shops and used-book stores. If your song is a golden oldie, pop into **Rockin' Al's Music and Vintage Stuff** (3586-A Adams Avenue; 619–282–0675). **Back from Tomboctou Gallery & Imports** (3564 Adams Avenue; 619–282–8708) features exotic items from around the globe. Seeking a hard-to-find, out-of-print book? Try **Adams Avenue Book Store** (3502 Adams Avenue; 619–281–3330). Old treasures seek new owners at **Refindery Antiques & Collectibles** (3463 Adams Avenue; 619–563–0655).

At the far east end of Adams Avenue you'll arrive in Kensington, one of San Diego's wonderful, understated old neighborhoods. Park and walk north of Adams to explore gracious streets of lovingly maintained red-tile-roofed, adobe Spanish-style homes, most built in the 1920s and '30s. Continue east and you'll run into the residential area of Talmadge, named after silent film star Norma Talmadge and her sisters, who used to own the subdivision.

DAY ONE: *Evening*

DINNER

Kensington Grill (4055 Adams Avenue; 619–281–4014; moderate; reservations recommended) is one of those places that seems to satisfy everyone's needs. With friendly service, it's a popular hangout with the locals. But its warm, buttery yellow walls glow by candlelight, which makes it a wonderfully romantic spot, too. A creative menu with specialties like baby spinach salad with grilled walnuts, a spicy black linguini with rock shrimp, and a sublime grilled salmon makes Kensington Grill rate as a special night out. After dinner, retire to the bar area for a warming cognac or espresso.

Right next door to the restaurant is the **Ken Cinema** (4061 Adams Avenue; 619–283–5909), best known for screening revivals of old classics, cult favorites, and cutting-edge films you won't find at the multiplex. Check the schedule to see if you want to catch tonight's offering.

FOR MORE ROMANCE

If you're not quite ready to wind up the evening and want a nightcap, pop into the cozy and intimate **Wine Lover** (3968 Fifth Avenue; 619–294–9200; inexpensive). This wine bar specializes in California vintages—perfect to toast your bond.

Courtship on the Water
MARINA SERENADE

AN DIEGO INTERNATIONAL AIRPORT AT LINDBERGH FIELD must rank as one of the best situated and prettiest locations for any airport in the world. Sitting on prime waterfront acreage, Lindbergh Field overlooks glittering San Diego Bay and the endless sea of yachts and small sailboats. From Navy aircraft carriers to commercial fishing vessels to America's Cup-winning yachts, boating is an integral part of San Diego's culture. This laid-back itinerary highlights that nautical romance.

PRACTICAL NOTES: One drawback to this trip: since it's so close to the airport, you'll find yourself in the flight path, which means that throughout the day your romantic idyll is subject to the roar of planes coming and going. However, once you've tuned out that interference (and you do get used to it), you'll discover the area's charms. For more waterfront fun, link this trip with Itinerary 5 to Mission Beach and Bay.

DAY ONE: *Morning*

The highlight of this trip is a unique overnight stay aboard a private yacht, sailboat or floating villa, so make your way to the **San Diego Yacht & Breakfast Company** (Marina Cortez, 1880 Harbor Island Drive, G Dock; 800–922–4836; $185–$195). The vessels differ in size and amenities, but all offer a unique twist on the bed-and-breakfast concept. All the boats feature natural wood interiors, a large salon, private aft deck, and a stocked galley where you can prepare your own meals. The luxury berths easily compare to a five-star hotel room. You'll have access to marina facilities, too,

Romance
AT A GLANCE

* Yachts may be a rich man's hobby, but you can live the good life for a night aboard a private yacht, sailboat, or floating villa with **San Diego Yacht & Breakfast Company** (Marina Cortez, 1880 Harbor Island Drive, G Dock; 800–922–4836).

* Admire sweeping views of the Pacific and San Diego Bay from high atop **Cabrillo National Monument** (Cabrillo Memorial Drive; 619–557–5450). In winter, you may also spot migrating gray whales.

* Share a casual lunch by the marina at **Point Loma Seafoods** (2805 Emerson Street; 619–223–1109).

* Learn how to tack and row with a lesson at the **San Diego Sailing Club** (Marina Cortez, 1880 Harbor Island Drive; 619–298–6623).

* Have a romantic dinner and maybe catch a show at **Humphrey's Half Moon Inn and Suites** (2303 Shelter Island Drive; 800–345–9995). Headline entertainment, such as Ray Charles and Kenny G, performs every summer.

* After the concert, relax on the deck of your yacht and share a bottle of wine under the stars.

including a heated swimming pool and spa, health club, delicatessen, party room, and bike rentals.

Snag a couple of bikes to see the sights. Pedal over to Point Loma, where it's a good idea to start at the top and work your way down. It's a long, steady ride up to **Cabrillo National Monument** (end of Cabrillo Memorial Drive; 619–557–5420; $5.00 per car; $2.00 per bike), but the view at the top is worth the exertion. (If the two of you are not up to biking, you can always drive). This is as close to sacred ground in San Diego as you're likely to get. In 1542, Juan Rodriguez Cabrillo sailed around this rocky peninsula and became the first European to set eyes on the West Coast. The Spanish conquistador's statue continues to scan the horizon from this windswept spot. He has the right idea. From here you can see it all— the endless Pacific, all of San Diego Bay, and the downtown skyline. It's come a long way from the chaparral-covered hills Cabrillo claimed for Spain.

Just a stroll away from the monument is the **Old Point Loma Lighthouse,** which started operation in 1855. This plain, white-washed building looks like it belongs in an Edward Hopper painting. It's also a great spot for whale watching during the December-through-March season. Bring binoculars, or rent them from the park rangers, to glimpse Pacific gray whales on their annual migration south to Baja California. During the peak month of January, as many as 200 whales have been sighted in a single day.

There also are terrific hiking trails throughout the park. The short **Bayside Trail** begins next to the lighthouse. At low tide, investigate the **Point Loma Tide Pools** (Catalina Boulevard; 619–557–5450), in which abalone, anemones, and other sea creatures carve out their precarious existence.

DAY ONE: *Afternoon*

LUNCH

You'll find a plethora of seafood places in Point Loma. One of the best deals in town is at **Point Loma Seafoods** (2805 Emerson Street; 619–223–1109; inexpensive). It's standing room only at lunchtime, when hungry patrons line up six deep at the counter. Just queue up and peruse the menu. Their fried fish sandwiches on sourdough bread are a decadent treat; so are their fish tacos. When your order comes up, take your food outside to one of the tables by the dock. You'll be serenaded by the lapping waves, boats groaning in their moorings, and squawking seagulls overhead.

There are two major areas for exploring the marinas: Shelter Island and Harbor Island. These minipeninsulas are host to the big hotels and marinas. Here you can walk or cycle by the swaying masts of the yachts and catamarans. If you want to dabble on the water, rent a boat at the **San Diego Sailing Club** (Marina Cortez, 1880 Harbor Island Drive; 619–298–6623; $70 for four hours). On neighboring Shelter Island you can relax under the bougainvillea-laced trellises at **Shoreline Park** (1500 Shelter Island Drive; 619–686–6200) at the north end of the island.

DAY ONE: *Evening*

One of the landmark entertainment locations in San Diego is the unassuming **Humphrey's Half Moon Inn and Suites** on Shelter Island (2303 Shelter Island Drive; 800–345–9995). Humphrey's has become one of the premiere nightspots in town with its annual Concerts by the Bay (June through October). This intimate spot is the place to get up close and personal with some of the biggest names in entertainment. Ray Charles, Bill Cosby, Kenny G, and Ringo Starr are some of the headliners who have performed at Humphrey's. Tickets for these events usually sell out, however, so plan accordingly.

DINNER

Even if you're not catching a show, Humphrey's is a great spot for a romantic dinner. With its tropical landscaping and its views overlooking the bay

with the glittering backdrop of the San Diego skyline beyond, this is a hands down winner for location. The menu offers seafood, large salads and pastas with Caribbean, Mediterranean, and Pacific Rim flavors, as well as the traditional American steaks and lobster.

End your evening over a bottle of wine and candles on the deck of your private *Love Boat*.

DAY TWO: *Morning*

BREAKFAST

Your stay with San Diego Yacht & Breakfast comes with a breakfast voucher at the marina deli. Flip a coin to decide who gets to sleep in and who has to nip over to the deli to fetch breakfast and a morning paper.

FOR MORE ROMANCE

Want to live the romance of a fishing adventure and battle the big one at sea, à la Ernest Hemingway? **Point Loma Sportfishing** (1403 Scott Street; 619-223-1627; $25 per person) has half-day excursions that leave bright and early at 6:00 A.M. The trip takes you out to the Coronado Islands, where you will angle for a wide variety of exotic fish. Maybe you'll hook a barracuda.

JOSHUA TREE NATIONAL PARK

Nature's Playground

Wild Things
THE SAN DIEGO ZOO AND SAN DIEGO WILD ANIMAL PARK

EW ACTIVITIES ARE MORE "SAN DIEGO" THAN A VISIT TO THE CITY'S WORLD-FAMOUS ZOO and the nearby Wild Animal Park. This two-day itinerary will give you plenty of time to explore both parks—each is a very different experience—with a relaxing evening in between.

Located in Balboa Park, the zoo is home to more than 4,000 animals, many of them rare and endangered species. If one of you is a green thumb, you'll enjoy an added treat—the zoo also is an accredited botanical garden filled with everything from eucalyptus and palm trees to rare orchids, fig trees, and coral trees. It's hard to imagine, but this was just a scrub-covered expanse of hills and canyons when it opened in 1922.

If your travel plans—and budget—don't allow for a safari to Africa any time soon, a trip to the San Diego Wild Animal Park is the next best thing. And it's only a forty-five-minute drive north of the zoo. This behemoth younger sister (at 2,200 acres it's more than twenty times the size of the zoo) is home to entire herds of antelope, gazelle, giraffes, water buffalo, rhinoceroses, and other beasts that contentedly roam through vast enclosures. Originally developed as a breeding facility for endangered species (a purpose it continues to fulfill admirably), the park opened to the public in 1972. Its environmentally sensitive habitats are unlike anything you'll see outside a bona fide game reserve—with one major exception: While some species share enclosures, much as they would in the wild, don't expect to see a cheetah take down a gazelle or a lion attack a warthog. The developers didn't go *that* far to re-create natural conditions.

PRACTICAL NOTES: For general information about the San Diego Zoo, call (619) 234–3153 or visit the zoo website at www.sandiegozoo.org. Call (888) 697–2632 for updates about the giant pandas on loan from China. The Wild Animal Park is inland, which means temperatures climb into the 90s during the summer. Dress accordingly, and don't forget sunglasses and high-SPF sunscreen. The sun is really bright, but hey, it just adds to the safari ambience. Comfortable walking shoes are a must to explore the zoo and the park. Bring a camera, too, since the flora and fauna are mighty photogenic. Since the Wild Animal Park's enclosures are enormous, a pair of binoculars (or even a camera with a telephoto lens) makes it easier to spot the animals.

DAY ONE:

Morning

The **San Diego Zoo** (Park Boulevard at Zoo Place; 619–234–3153) is one of the most convenient major attractions in the county. It's located in Balboa Park, just five minutes from downtown and the airport. Admission is $16 per person, but since you're going to the Wild Animal Park tomorrow, request a two-park admission pass for $35.15 per person.

The zoo's 100-plus acres cover canyons and mesas common to San Diego, which can mean some steep climbs. Purchase a pair of tickets for the narrated Kangaroo Bus Tour ($8.00 per person) from

Romance
AT A GLANCE

✷ Get an overview of the entire **San Diego Zoo** (Park Boulevard at Zoo Place; 619–234–3153) from the Skyfari Aerial Tramway which stretches across the treetops.

✷ Save your feet by taking the Kangaroo Bus Tour. You can hop on and off at eight designated stops throughout the zoo.

✷ Have lunch on the patio at **Albert's Restaurant,** the zoo's fine-dining option located in the Treehouse.

✷ Spend the night in the **Balboa Park Inn** (3402 Park Boulevard; 619–298–0823 or 800–938–8181), conveniently located 1 block from the zoo. Be sure to request the jungle-themed Greystoke suite.

✷ Have a quiet dinner at the **Parkhouse Eatery** (4574 Park Boulevard; 619–295–7275).

✷ Feed the exotic and friendly birds at Lorikeet Landing at the **San Diego Wild Animal Park** (15500 San Pasqual Road; 760–747–8702), and then see what the cheetahs are up to in the Heart of Africa.

✷ Offer snacks to a small herd of friendly Baringo giraffes—ask someone to snap of picture of the two of you with your new pals.

✷ Take the pictures of a lifetime aboard a **Photo Caravan** (760–738–5022).

the ticket booth to the right of the Flamingo Lagoon at the entrance. The bus makes a continuous circuit that covers 75 percent of the park, and you can get on and off at eight stops. If you forgot a camera or need extra film, pick up a single-use camera and other photo supplies at the Camera Den near the entrance.

You'll explore the first exhibits on foot. The entrance to Tiger River is to the left of the Flamingo Lagoon. This footpath winds through a lush Sumatran forest of tropical plants. Residents of this humid environment—kept appropriately moist with automatic misters—include gavials, a crocodile native to India, and, of course, tigers that you might catch at play in the water. Follow the Tiger River path down to Hippo Beach to watch these chubby, water-loving mammals in their aquatic element. Or make a detour into the Scripps Aviary, the spacious, verdant home to a variety of showy tropical birds.

From the aviary, it's a short stroll to the Gorilla Tropics, home a colony of majestic silver-backed lowland gorillas. These zoo residents always attract a crowd. After all, they seem (and in many ways are) similar to us, whether it's in the way the young 'uns gambol about their ever-patient mothers or the way the big daddy quietly contemplates the human visitors on the other side of the fence while keeping a watchful eye on his brood.

DAY ONE: *Afternoon*

LUNCH

Located in The Treehouse, near the Gorilla Tropics, **Albert's Restaurant** (moderate) is the zoo's upscale dining option. The restaurant is named for a silver-backed lowland gorilla who lived at the zoo from 1949 until his death in 1978. With the ambience of a safari lodge club dining room— wicker bistro chairs, plantation shutters, and ceiling fans—it's a fitting tribute to such a beloved and noble resident. Sit on the patio and you'll enjoy the soothing splash of a waterfall. It's delightful spot to refuel for the afternoon. Quaff a microbrew while choosing from an agreeable mix of entree-size salads, gourmet pizzas, fresh fish, and sandwiches. Indulge in dessert— maybe chocolate toffee mousse with Kahlua—since you'll easily walk off the excess calories.

After lunch, amble over to the Birds of Prey exhibit to glimpse bald eagles, vultures and other enormous raptors hanging out in the treetops.

From there you can hop on Stop 2 of the Kangaroo Bus route to the Polar Bear Plunge. Allow at least half an hour to take in this 2.2-acre exhibit, one of the largest in the world devoted to these bruins. Waterfowl and a herd of Siberian reindeer share their plush quarters, but the bears are the undisputed stars of this exhibit. Lounging on their backs, contentedly soaking up the San Diego sunshine, these huge, white beasts look as languid and cuddly as teddy bears. Of course, they could take off your head with one swipe of a mighty paw, so it's nice to know they're well fed and separated from you by 5 inches of acrylic glass. The bears love to show off their superb aquatic skills in their 130,000-gallon pool of chilled water. Be sure to pause in the arctic cave, where you can watch their underwater antics. Don't be surprised when they gracefully paddle up to the glass, take a gander at their human visitors, and execute a flip turn worthy of any Olympic swimmer.

From the Polar Bear Plunge, ride the Kangaroo Bus through the north end of the zoo as it meanders past the zebras, gazelles, giraffes, wild pigs, and big cats. Simply enjoy the view and lively commentary, or hop off at one of three stops along the way. In any case, you'll want to get off at Stop 7 for the Giant Panda Research Station. Exhibit hours for the pandas are limited and change daily, so check the schedule when you arrive at the zoo. High demand and limited hours mean visitors are herded through the exhibit at a snappy pace. Still, it's worth the chance to glimpse these black-and-white gentle giants on a twelve-year loan from the People's Republic of China. Most likely you'll see the male, Shi Shi, nestled in a corner nibbling on bamboo, while the female, Bai Yun, likes to climb into the trees for a nap. Scientists from the zoo's renowned Center for Reproducton of Endangered Species hope the pair will breed. However, pandas are nortoriously shy, and courtship in captivity is typically an awkward affair.

After visiting the pandas, you have two routes out of the canyon, depending on how tired you are. A speed ramp ferries you up to a pair of terrific aviaries, including one featuring exotic birds of the rain forest. Also check out the Southeast Asia Exhibit and orangutans' enclosure. If you don't mind an uphill trek, follow the path through the luxuriant Sun Bear Forest, which will deposit you at the entrance of Fern Canyon. In the midst of this Eden, you'll quickly forget that San Diego is a desert, and it's a pleasant rest stop.

If seeing the zoo's many residents makes you long for closer contact, head over to the Children's Zoo on the south end of the park. There you'll find the requisite petting corral, where you can stroke a gentle goat or sheep. Don't forget to stop by the nursery to welcome any newcomers.

The Children's Zoo is conveniently located next to the east terminal of the Skyfari Aerial Tramway. A round-trip ride ($1.00 per person, each way) is the perfect way to end your zoo expedition. You'll have one of these open-air gondolas all to yourselves as it glides over the treetops. It's a romantic overview of the zoo and all of Balboa Park. Gazing down, you won't believe how much ground you covered today.

DAY ONE: *Evening*

Check into your room at the **Balboa Park Inn** (3402 Park Boulevard; 619–298–0823 or 800–938–8181; $85–$200) at the end of the day, if you haven't already done so. It's located just around the corner from the zoo, so you won't have to go far. To keep up the animal theme, reserve the Greystoke suite. Animal-head masks adorn the walls, while a king-size canopy bed and a mirrored bathroom with a whirlpool tub for two offer a fine setting for a romantic evening.

DINNER

It's been a long day on your feet, so plan dinner at the nearby **Parkhouse Eatery** (4574 Park Boulevard; 619–295–7275; moderate). You'll find a menu of self-described "American ethnic grub"—a quirky mélange of spicy pastas, great homemade soups, and salmon served on a cedar plank in unpretentious surroundings. Request a table by the fireplace, or if it's a pleasant evening, dine under the fairy lights on the front patio.

DAY TWO: *Morning*

BREAKFAST

Start your day with the complimentary continental breakfast served in the privacy of your room.

After breakfast, pull your stuff together, check out, and hit the road to the San Diego Wild Animal Park, which is nestled in North County's San Pasqual Valley. Once you leave the freeway, you're treated to views of the county's rugged backcountry. Just follow the signs from Interstate 15 to the **San Diego Wild Animal Park** (15500 San Pasqual Road; 760–747–8702). Parking is $3.00.

Take a moment to peruse the park map and get the lay of this vast attraction. You could easily spend the day just exploring the 17-acre Nairobi Village, which has a number of exhibits, dining options, and, of course, gift shops. Instead, amble along a footpath that winds along the Mombassa Lagoon, which teems with wildlife—abundant waterfowl, ring-tailed lemurs performing their stunts, a family of lowland gorillas. Don't miss the Hidden Jungle, a greenhouse that's also home to exotic birds and gloriously vivid butterflies (wear bright clothes to attract these delicate, winged creatures). Next to that is Lorikeet Landing. Buy some food to hand-feed these congenial birds, whose jewel-tone red, purple, green, and yellow feathers make a marvelous photo opportunity.

Follow the path as it goes down a steep trail to the park's newest feature, the 30-acre Heart of Africa. Pick up a free field guide at the entrance so you can identify the diverse population of birds, antelope, rhinoceroses, and other wildlife. Designed to make visitors feel like explorers, the expedition theme is carried out with a simulated research station, where a resident researcher brings over some of the wildlife for closer inspection. As you amble along paths over floating walkways, you'll notice that this cleverly conceived attraction puts animals in close proximity to visitors. Reigning over all this are the South African cheetahs. You'll likely spot two or three snoozing on the ridge—their favorite activity until a sudden sound in the distance makes them snap to attention.

You'll enjoy a close encounter with other Heart of Africa residents. With their lanky elegance and enormous, long-lashed brown eyes, the Baringo giraffes are surely the sweethearts of Africa. Buy some food from a dispenser and hand-feed these beauties. One or two will surely saunter up to daintily accept your offering. These giraffes are so docile that park staffers have to remind visitors not to pet them. Indeed, it's hard to resist the urge to stroke a snout or pat a long neck.

DAY TWO: *Afternoon*

LUNCH

For lunch, relax on the terrace at **Okavango Outpost** (inexpensive) in the Heart of Africa. The menu is a pedestrian mix of salads, sandwiches, and hot dogs, but you can't beat the view.

Thus refueled, you'll be ready to take on the Kilimanjaro Safari Walk, a 1.75-mile footpath that skirts a mesa overlooking the immense East Africa

enclosure. Take a break at Kilima Point to rest your feet and peer through the telescopes at the animals below. Continue your stroll over a suspension bridge to the Tiger Overlook. You'll have to look closely to spot the Sumatran tigers slumbering among the trees, because their striped coats blend into the dappled sunlight. African lions occupy a large adjacent enclosure, but their sandy coats are even more difficult to spy in the dun-colored hills. It takes a sharp eye, not to mention plenty of patience.

Amateur horticulturists will want to extend their stroll into the park's **Botanical Gardens**. This 1.25-mile trail (easily cut short to suit your time and interest) takes you from a Protea Garden through a Conifer Garden and into areas devoted to succulents and native plants. Pause at the Kupanda Falls Botanical Pavilion to enjoy the serene surroundings.

Love in the Bush

The San Diego Wild Animal Park's natural setting is ideal for animal romance and has led to lots of offspring. Vast enclosures mean that antelope, rhinoceroses, and other animals have plenty of space to form natural herds and even harems for breeding. The park's greatest success story has been the California Condor Recovery Project. The first park-bred condors were released into the wild in 1991. Half the condors alive today were hatched at the Wild Animal Park.

After exploring so much on foot, it's time to take a break. Much of the park's 2,200 acres can be seen only from the Wgasa Bush Line Monorail. This electric train was designed to glide silently through the animals' habitats, which are 60 to 100 acres in size. The 5-mile, hour-long trip is a must. It's your opportunity to spot an endangered rhinoceros (the park has the largest rhino population outside Asia and Africa) lumbering up to the watering hole or a clutch of gazelles napping in the shade. What's most striking about the park isn't necessarily the size of its enclosures, which is remarkable, but the way several species share the space, much as they would on their native savannas.

A more deluxe way to get even closer to the animals is aboard a **Photo Caravan** (760–738–5022; reservations are a must). Riding in an open pickup truck, amateur shutterbugs snap first-rate close-ups of Baringo giraffes, Kenyan impalas, Thompson's gazelles, endangered white rhinos, and other beasts that roam these vast enclosures. You'd have to pop for an

African safari to get better pictures. Two-hour trips are $65 per person, including park admission, the monorail ride, and parking; a more extensive version lasts three and a half hours and costs $89 per person.

FOR MORE ROMANCE

Visiting in summer? The San Diego Zoo is open until 9:00 P.M., and the evening hours are the best time to see the resident night owls strut their stuff. Tigers, leopards, lions, and other big cats prowl under the cloak of darkness, while the moonlight is a cuddly koala's cue to rise and shine (the zoo has the largest colony of koalas outside their native Australia).

At the Wild Animal Park, you can experience the veldt by moonlight with a Night Moves tour. You'll explore the park's enclosures by moonlight, followed by a medley of desserts and a lively lecture about animal courtship. It's $150 per couple; call 760–738–5057 for reservations. If you want an abbreviated safari experience, sign up for one of the park's Roar & Snore Camp-Overs, offered Friday and Saturday nights from April through October. With guided hikes at dusk and dawn, hearty gourmet meals cooked over an open fire, and gazelles and giraffes roaming below, you'll feel like you're really on a bluff overlooking the East African savanna. Call (760) 738–5049 or (800) 934–2267 to get dates for adult-only camps (other camp-overs are more family oriented). Camps are $87.50 per person, including park admission after 4:00 P.M., private tent accommodations (you provide the sleeping bags), dinner, campfire snacks, a pancake breakfast, and park admission the following day.

On the way home from the Wild Animal Park, you can stop at **Orfila Vineyards and Winery** (13455 San Pasqual Road; 760–738–6500). From the road, you can see acres of vines neatly planted on the rolling landscape. The area's balmy climate produces some award-winning red wines, which you can sample at the vineyard's tasting room, open daily from 10:00 A.M. to 6:00 P.M. Relax on a shady patio with a lovely view of the vineyards.

Apple Pie Pleasures
JULIAN'S SLICE OF THE OLD WEST

NEWCOMERS ALWAYS ACCUSE SOUTHERN CALIFORNIA of having an endless summer. Residents will say you simply haven't stayed long enough to sense the subtle changes in season. Then they point to the tiny mountain hamlet of Julian as evidence that there are, indeed, four seasons in San Diego. At 4,235 feet above sea level, this onetime mining town offers colorful leaves in fall; snow-covered winter landscapes; a fragrant profusion of daffodils and lilacs in the spring; and hiking, mountain biking, and fishing in the summer.

Julian enjoyed a brief heyday as a mining town after gold was discovered in 1870 in the surrounding hills. The same year, the first apple trees were planted in the area. Those gold mines have long been abandoned, but acres of orchards produce modern-day gold in the form of prized Julian apples that are pressed into cider and baked into pies every fall. Whether you visit Julian during the busy fall season—or any time—you'll find its lazy pace is ideal for an intimate escape. As you lounge in a hammock and listen to the wind rustle through the manzanita trees and the distant cry of an eagle, everyday cares will seem light-years away. If Julian weaves its languid spell and you simply can't rouse yourselves for a hike or bike ride, just relax, open a bottle of local wine, and know this getaway is going as planned.

PRACTICAL NOTES: Fall is prime time in Julian, when San Diegans make their annual pilgrimage to enjoy the autumn nip in the air,

admire the fall colors and, of course, gorge on apple pie. Fall weekends are very crowded, so definitely plan a midweek getaway. There are more than two dozen inns, cabins, and B&Bs in the area. Contact the **Julian Bed & Breakfast Guild** (760–765–1555 or www.julianbnb.com) for a listing. Remember, most inns require a two-night minimum for weekends and holidays. Call the **Julian Chamber of Commerce** (760–765–1857; www.julianca.com) to request a helpful visitor's guide. For updates on local attractions and events, call the **Julian Info Center** at 760–786–0707. For more time away from the daily grind, combine this trip with Itinerary 17 to Anza-Borrego Desert State Park. The park is just 30 minutes east of Julian on Highway 78, and its wide-open desert vistas are a remarkable contrast to Julian's pine-cloaked mountains.

DAY ONE: *Afternoon*

Half the fun of going to Julian is the drive getting there. From San Diego take Interstate 8 east to Highway 67. Follow this north through the backcountry towns of Lakeside and Ramona. In Ramona catch Highway 78 east toward Julian. This two-lane highway meanders through Santa Ysabel Valley, past small herds of cattle and roadside diners. In Santa Ysabel stop for a cup of coffee and a doughnut at **Dudley's Bakery** (Highway 78 and 79; 760–765–0488; inexpensive). In an age of chichi patisseries, this local landmark is a comforting throwback to a simpler time. The decor is basic-bakery, but no one minds waiting in line for a loaf of fresh date-nut-raisin bread or a medley of doughnuts and turnovers.

Romance
AT A GLANCE

⁎ Enjoy the scenic drive through San Diego's rugged backcountry to this tiny town nestled in the mountains.

⁎ Stay at the deluxe **Orchard Hill Country Inn** (2502 Washington Street; 760–765–1700 or 800–716–7242), just a block from the heart of town, or for more quiet isolation, rent a cabin at the **Artists' Loft**, the **Cabin at Strawberry Hill,** and **Big Cat Cabin** (4811 Pine Ridge Avenue; 760–765–0765; www.artist-sloft.com).

⁎ Stroll along Julian's historic Main Street and sample the apple pie at **Mom's Pies, Etc.** (2119 Main Street; 760–765–2472).

⁎ Pack a picnic and spend the afternoon hiking in **Volcan Mountain Wilderness Preserve.**

⁎ Sample the vintages at **Menghini Winery** (1150 Julian Orchards Drive; 760–765–2072).

⁎ Unwind with an in-room massage for two.

After your pilgrimage to Dudley's, walk up the street to the **Santa Ysabel Art Gallery** (30352 Highway 78; 760–765–1676), where owner Annie Rowley showcases first-rate work by local artists (no country kitsch here). The light-filled, airy space is an ideal backdrop for fanciful metalwork, pottery, and paintings; don't be surprised if you find a well-priced piece that just has to come home with you. Gallery hours are Wednesday through Sunday, from 10:00 A.M. to 1:00 P.M. and from 2:00 P.M. to 5:00 P.M.

The Real McCoy

Other towns may play up their Old West past, but Julian is genuine. The town was established by ex-Confederate soldier-cum-prospector Drury Bailey, who named the new settlement after his cousin, Mike Julian, a devilishly handsome ladies' man. Today you'll find Bailey and Julian's other founding fathers laid to rest in the serene old Pioneer Cemetery off A Street. Shaded by oak and pine trees, the hilltop plot looks just like the graveyards in old Westerns.

From Santa Ysabel, continue east on Highway 78 as it steadily climbs into Julian. You're in mountain country now, surrounded by pine, oak, and manzanita trees. Dozens of inns, B&Bs, and cabins dot the hills in and around Julian. Both charming and deluxe, **Orchard Hill Country Inn** (2502 Washington Street; 760–765–1700 or 800–716–7242; www.orchardhill.com; $132–$225) is a quiet retreat just steps from Julian's shops and restaurants. Owners Pat and Darrell Staube opened Orchard Hill in 1994 as a reproduction of a California Craftsman lodge, and they haven't missed a romantic touch. In-room amenities include a half-bottle of local Witch Creek Winery merlot, a Mason jar filled with freshly baked oatmeal cookies, silky-soft robes, current magazines, and a basket of games to while away a rainy afternoon. You'll also find private benches, rockers, and hammocks tucked among the inn's tree-filled four acres. Ten delightful rooms are in the main lodge, but for a truly romantic getaway, reserve one of the twelve cottage suites. Each is individually decorated and named for an apple variety, such as the softly feminine Sweet Bough suite or the more tailored (but no less cozy) warm plaids of McIntosh. If you visit in fall or winter, request a room with a fireplace and whirlpool tub.

A more isolated spot is the eleven-acre compound at the **Artists' Loft,** the **Cabin at Strawberry Hill,** and **Big Cat Cabin** (4811 Pine Ridge Avenue; 760–765–0765; www.artistsloft.com; $115–$145), the ongoing, environmentally sensitive creation of artists Nanessence and Chuck Kimball. Two

rooms in the Artists' Loft are decorated with a colorful, eclectic jumble of rustic antiques, Persian rugs, and the Kimballs' artwork. Next door, the Cabin at Strawberry Hill was hand-built by the couple. It features a blue-tin roof and is named for the wild strawberries that flourish nearby. A wood-burning stove keeps this spacious cabin warm even in winter, while a screened-in porch lets you enjoy the outdoors—without the bugs. At night bud lights along the deck set an appropriately romantic mood. The Kimballs' latest project is Big Cat Cabin, a lovingly restored, seventy-year-old cabin, complete with a wood stall shower, a claw-foot tub, a stone fireplace, a huge antique Balinese wedding bed, and a screened-in study.

After checking into your lodgings, unwind for a bit, then head over to **Julian Stables** ($35 per person; by reservation only; 760–765–1598) for a ninety-minute guided sunset ride in the hills outside town. Groups are small, and if you want it to be just the two of you and a guide, that's fine, too. The hilly route follows quiet dirt roads and deserted single-track trails with views of Volcan Mountain and the three peaks of the Cuyamaca Mountains. You'll get some idea of the glorious solitude and beauty that moved town founder Drury Bailey to settle in the area.

DAY ONE: *Evening*

DINNER

Return to the inn to rinse off the trail dust, then head to **Julian Grille** (2224 Main Street; 760–765–0173; reservations recommended; moderate to expensive). Frankly, Julian isn't known for great cuisine, and Julian Grille offers the best dining available (aside from the guests-only dinners served a few times a week at Orchard Hill). Your best bet is a simply prepared dish—say, a steak or grilled seafood. What the restaurant lacks in gastronomic flair, it makes up in ambience. When the weather is mild, request an outdoor table under the stars. If it's nippy, the tables scattered throughout the former private home have a charming, old-timey feel that's just right in this casual mountain town.

After dinner don't expect wild nightlife—Julian seems to roll up its sidewalks (what few there are) by 8:00 P.M. On weekends you might find live music, from country ditties to '60s rock tunes, at the big red barn of **Bailey Barbecue** (2307 Main Street; 760–765–2532). Otherwise, stargazing is by far the best show in town. Far from the city lights and with few streetlights to interfere, the celestial show is spec-

tacular. Most of the time the twinkling sky offers a shooting star or two. In August and December meteor showers light up the night sky.

DAY TWO: *Morning*

BREAKFAST

Sleep in, then linger over a hearty breakfast at your inn. At Orchard Hill freshbaked muffins and a hot dish (maybe vegetable quiche or sweetly decadent stuffed French toast) are served on the patio or in a tranquil dining room with a mural depicting the surrounding hillsides. After breakfast ask for a sumptuous picnic lunch ($20 for two), which consists of fresh fruit, sausage, gourmet cheese, homemade rolls, fresh oatmeal cookies, and apple cider or local wine.

Spend the rest of the morning exploring the town on foot. The original false-front buildings that line Main Street may look like the set of a Western movie, but these are the real thing. The oldest date back to 1871, and where butchers' shops, general stores, banks, and other businesses once served the booming mining town, today you'll find boutiques and cafes catering to Julian's bustling tourist trade. Plaques on the buildings offer the details, but don't miss the **Julian Drug Store** (2134 Main Street; 760–765–0332), which houses the **Miner's Diner**. The attraction here is an old-fashioned soda fountain, where you can claim a couple of stools at the marble counter and share a root beer float.

If you can't get enough of Old West history, wander through the **Julian Pioneer Museum** (2811 Washington Street; 760–765–0227; $1.00 donation). It's a little like meandering through your grandpa's attic—if he was a crusty old miner, that is. Local residents donated many of the items on display, which range from antique lace and old clothes (worn by departmentstore mannequins) to stuffed wildlife residents (raccoons, mountain lions, and the like), rusty mining tools, and scads of old photographs.

After that you'll be ready for a slice of Julian apple pie and a cup of coffee. Virtually every cafe claims to have the best pie in town, but locals gravitate toward **Mom's Pies, Etc.** (2119 Main Street; 760–765–2472) or the **Julian Pie Company** (2225 Main Street; 760–765–2449). After sharing a slice—a la mode, of course—you're sure to agree.

Claim your picnic lunch back at the inn, or stock up on supplies at the **Julian Market and Deli** (corner of Main and Washington). At least swing by the market to pick up some bottled water, because you'll spend the afternoon on the trails.

DAY TWO: *Afternoon*

Drive two miles out of town north on Farmers Road, hang a right on Wynola Road, then another left to pick up Farmers Road once again. Look for the sign for the **Volcan Mountain Wilderness Preserve** (760–765–2811) on your right. Park on the street, then walk up a private gravel road, past apple orchards to the trailhead. You can't miss it—it's the most elaborate trail marker you'll ever see. Local artist James Hubbell designed this fanciful stone and carved-wood creation depicting the wild residents who live in the preserve—rabbits, raccoons, snakes. And mountain lions. Yes, these majestic beasts call Julian home. Since you're hiking together, you're not likely to be bothered. If you do encounter a mountain lion, stand tall, wave, shout, and make plenty of noise. A 1.2-mile path winds halfway up the mountain. Views of the rolling hills, Cuyamaca Mountains, and the town of Julian nestled in the trees below are worth the trek. Besides, the effort will help you burn off that slice of apple pie. Any huffing and puffing isn't just a result of the vigorous hike, but the altitude. By the end of the trail, you'll be at more than 5,000 feet above sea level.

Find a pleasant spot under a shady oak or manzanita tree to enjoy your picnic, or stroll down the mountain, hop back in the car, and drive over to **Menghini Winery** (1150 Julian Orchards Drive; 760–765–2072; open daily 10:00 A.M. to 4:00 P.M.). From Volcan Mountain, head back out Farmers Road, turn right on Wynola Road, then right again on Julian Orchards Drive. Housed in a former apple-packing house, the winery offers free samples of its chardonnay, sauvignon blanc, and Julian Blossom Gamay beaujolais. You can purchase a bottle of your favorite vintage to enjoy with your picnic at the tree-shaded tables out back.

You've been on your feet a lot today and deserve a little tender loving care. Debbie Fetterman (619–637–8611; $130 for two) offers an in-room, two-hour **massage and aromatherapy treatment** for couples. While you wait your turn for Fetterman's treatment, sip the champagne she brings along with her massage table.

DAY TWO: *Evening*

DINNER

At Orchard Hill, Pat Staube serves a delightful four-course prix-fixe dinner (moderate) in the guests-only dining room two to three nights a week. Make

reservations for this, since it's the best food in town. Menus change, but you might find an appetizer of prosciutto and melon; a salad of mixed greens and Gorgonzola cheese; grilled beef tenderloin with garlic mashed potatoes and grilled vegetables; and Orchard Hill's bread pudding for dessert. Not staying at Orchard Hill? Try **Romano's Dodge House** (2718 B Street; 760–765–1003; inexpensive) for Italian fare. Reservations recommended.

DAY THREE: *Morning*

Julian is glorious early in the morning, and you can greet the day with a gentle hike. From Orchard Hill or the end of C Street, take a five-minute walk along a dirt path that leads to the long-abandoned **George Washington Mine**. The mine itself is a mesh-covered hole in the side of the mountain, but this is where gold was discovered in 1870, and you can easily imagine the salty old miners who came to the area in search of their fortune. Nearby you'll find a reconstructed assay office and a blacksmith shop filled with old tools.

BREAKFAST

No doubt you've worked up an appetite for breakfast back at the inn. Afterward relax at the inn and savor a quiet morning. Or walk into town to check out a few shops and stock up on picnic supplies for the drive home (don't forget a couple of slices of pie to go). Then fill up the tank and take another route back into the city. Follow Highway 79 south out of Julian. This route takes you through Cuyamaca Rancho State Park and around Lake Cuyamaca, where you can rent a canoe to explore.

FOR MORE ROMANCE

Explore the area by hoof. **Country Carriages** (760–765–1471) picks up passengers in front of the Julian Drug Store on the corner of Main and Washington streets. Carriage tours of the small Historic District are $5.00 per person; half-mile rides into the country are $20.00 per couple.

Learn more about Julian's gold-mining history on a tour of the **Eagle Mining Company** (C Street, eight blocks northeast of Main; 760–765–0036). Tours, offered daily 9:00 A.M. to 3:00 P.M., are $7.00 per person.

Horse Whispering Country
RAMONA AND WARNER SPRINGS

I F THE TWO OF YOU NEED TO GET AWAY FROM IT ALL, Ramona offers an easy escape from the pressures of city life. It is San Diego County's own "horse whisper" country, home to countless ranches that raise and train racehorses. It's also a farming community that doesn't really cater to the tourist trade, which means no fancy resorts out here. Ramona is where you go to slow things down a bit, unwind in a bucolic setting, and experience a different way of life. This two-night itinerary has you sample two very different properties. Four-room Lake Sutherland Lodge is tucked in the hills between Ramona and Julian, while Warner Springs Ranch is a private resort once frequented by the likes of Gary Cooper, Charlie Chaplin, and Clark Gable.

PRACTICAL NOTES: Plan a midweek getaway if you want to join Warner Springs Llama Hikes for an outing (available Wednesday through Friday). This inland community can get very warm in the summertime, so your best bet is to make this trip during the period from fall through spring. In fact, the town hosts the famous Ramona Rodeo every May. The event draws more than 10,000 cowboys, ranchers, and fans. Any time of year, dress is strictly "cowboy-casual," so pack accordingly. If your wardrobe includes boots and a string tie, bring 'em along. You'll fit right in, pardners.

DAY ONE: *Afternoon*

Ramona is an easy forty-minute drive from San Diego. Just take Interstate 15 north to the Poway Road exit (Highway 67) and head east. The residential

Romance

AT A GLANCE

✳ *Meander through the antique shops along Ramona's historic Main Street. Wander through the **Guy B. Woodward Museum** (745 Main Street; 760–789–7644), which features a collection of turn-of-the century memorabilia.*

✳ *Spend your first night at the four-room **Lake Sutherland Lodge** (Dam Oaks Drive; 760–789–6483 or 800–789–6483). It's tucked on a lakeside meadow 6 miles out of town.*

✳ *Have a country dinner at **D'Carlo's** (1347 Main Street; 760–789–4340).*

✳ *Start the next day with a filling gourmet breakfast served on the deck overlooking Lake Sutherland.*

✳ *Enjoy an afternoon trekking along the trails in the company of friendly llamas with **Warner Springs Llama Hikes** (909– 767–0172). Let the mild-mannered llamas tote your lunch.*

✳ *Spend your second night at the secluded **Warner Springs Ranch** (31652 Highway 79; 760–782–4200).*

✳ *Occupy your final morning with taking advantage of some of the ranch's facilities. Ride horses, soak in the natural hot springs, or swing a club on the eighteen-hole golf course.*

community of Poway quickly gives way to the countryside. The winding Highway 67 turns into Ramona's Main Street. As the two of you approach Ramona you'll pass the wide-open, flat pastures of the horse ranches. Head on into the main part of town and you'll enter what resembles a Wild West main street. It's not an affectation to attract tourists, but a genuine legacy of what Ramona was—and still is.

Main Street runs for several blocks and is the center of activity in town. Park the car and mosey around for spell. A stroll up the street brings you face-to-face with history. **Ramona Friend's Church** (825 Main Street; 760–789–1844) dates back to 1893—pretty darned old for this neck of the woods. A little further along is the **Guy B. Woodward Museum** (745 Main Street; 760–789–7644; open Friday to Sunday, 1:00–4:00 P.M.; $3.00 per person). The French-country-style adobe house is a time capsule filled with clothing, furniture, and utensils from turn-of-the-century Ramona, complete with an authentic millinery shop and blacksmith's workshop. Ramona also bills itself as the antiques capital of San Diego, and you'll find more than a dozen shops along Main Street. Two to investigate are the **Victoria Supply Company** (711 Main Street; 760–789–5656) and **Ye Olde Curio Shoppe** (738 Main Street; 760–789–6365).

After nosing around Ramona, drive 6 miles northeast of town and check into **Lake Sutherland Lodge** (Dam Oaks Drive; 760–789–6483 or 800–789–6483; www.lolodge.com; $110–$205). This breathtaking mountain lodge retreat was built in 1994 and has plenty of rustic touches—lodge pole logs from Montana, a huge stone fireplace in the great room—along with the voluptuous amenities modern couples need for a romantic retreat. You don't have to be

A Literary Legacy

Ramona may have all the trappings of a cowpunk town, but it has a literary pedigree, too. The town was first settled by American Indians and came under Mexican rule in the early 1800s. Onetime landowner Milton Santee gave the town its name in honor of his favorite book, Helen Hunt Jackson's historic novel Ramona. *Silent-screen director D. W. Griffith made the romantic tale of an Indian maiden into a movie with Mary Pickford in 1910. Don Ameche and Loretta Young later starred in a 1936 version.*

newlyweds to enjoy the spacious Honeymoon Suite. Its king-size canopy bed and lace-covered sofa look like something out of a romance novel. The other three rooms have cozy feather beds, overstuffed chairs, and spectacular lake views. It's no surprise that this small, romantic retreat is a popular wedding spot.

DAY ONE: *Evening*

DINNER

As the clear blue skies give way to the darkness of night, head into Ramona for a romantic supper. Being a small country town, Ramona doesn't have the fancy high-end restaurants of the big city. But **D'Carlo's** (1347 Main Street; 760–789–4340; moderate) offers a wide variety of prime rib, steaks, and fresh fish dishes served in a quaint setting. In keeping with Ramona's equine theme, the restaurant even features a black horse etched into glass windows.

Back at the lodge, you can look to the skies for heavenly stargazing. Or just snuggle by the warmth of your suite's stone fireplace.

DAY TWO: *Morning*

BREAKFAST

Wake up together to the aroma of freshly brewed coffee. Breakfast, served on a deck overlooking Lake Sutherland, is a hearty gourmet repast that

might include cream cheese blintzes with fresh raspberries, followed by the lodge's signature Sutherland Eggs Benedict garnished with fresh herbs and seasonal flowers plucked from the garden.

There's no need to rush, but you will want to check out after breakfast. About twenty minutes east of Ramona lie the desert highlands of Warner Springs. Take Highway 78 east to Santa Ysabel, then swing north on Highway 79 to Warner Springs.

For a truly unique romantic adventure, join a llama train with **Warner Springs Llama Hikes**. Available from **Trailhead & Company** (30002 Chihuahua Valley Road; 909–767–0172) on Wednesdays, Thursdays, and Fridays (call ahead for reservations), the excursion takes you on the scenic trails of Warner Springs with a pair of gentle llamas for company. The trails are relatively short (just under 2 miles), but you'll spend three or four hours exploring the varied terrain—an oak forest, a willow creek bed, and a waterfall. Hikes cost $45 per person, including a gourmet lunch with dessert and drinks. The highlight, of course, is getting to know your new, four-hoofed pals. These endearing, slightly daft-looking beasts are beloved for their sweet nature. They're hardworking, too, since they'll tote your lunch for the day.

DAY TWO: *Afternoon*

For the second night of this itinerary you'll check in at **Warner Springs Ranch** (31652 Highway 79; 760–782–4200; $220). Situated at 3,000 feet in the foothills of Palomar Mountain, the ranch is one of the best-kept secrets in San Diego County. Dating back to 1844, the historic ranch was originally a stop on the Butterfield Overland Stage route. Exhausted travelers paused here for a refreshing dip in the ranch's natural hot springs. Early guests included presidents Teddy Roosevelt and Ulysses S. Grant. The famous Kit Carson visited, too. Later, the ranch became a Hollywood hot spot, entertaining the likes of Mary Pickford, Douglas Fairbanks, Charlie Chaplin, Gary Cooper, Clark Gable, Jean Harlow, John Wayne, and Bing Crosby. Today, the 234-room ranch is a private resort, but nonmembers can stay if they book one of the four packages available. Starting at $220 a night, these are a nice bargain. The spa package, for example, includes an hour-long massage for each of you, accommodations in a cozy room with a fireplace, and three meals. Other packages offer golf, tennis, or horseback riding.

Those natural hot springs that drew early stagecoach travelers still work their healing magic today. After settling into your room, slip into your bathing suits and soak away your cares in mineral baths nestled in an oasis shaded by lovely date palms.

DAY TWO: *Evening*

DINNER

After your day hiking with the llamas and soaking in the mineral pools, you'll be ready for dinner at the ranch's award-winning **Anza Dining Room**. Executive Chef Michel Malecot serves up a gourmet menu of Continental favorites. His menu changes weekly, but you can expect to find such entrees as potato-crusted salmon with Parmesan pesto and garlic-roasted leg of lamb with rosemary au jus. After dinner, you may want to share a nightcap in the Cantina lounge, or just gaze at the stars from the privacy of your bungalow's patio.

DAY THREE: *Morning*

BREAKFAST

Morning at Warner Springs Ranch is especially pleasant, so get up and head to the **Country Club Grill** for an early breakfast. Order an all-American repast of eggs with sausage, ham, or smokehouse bacon. Got a really big appetite? Opt for a three-egg omelette filled with spicy Mexican chorizo sausage.

After breakfast you can take advantage of the activity covered by your package. Take a couple of horses from the equestrian center to explore some of the ranch's 2,400 acres of scenic trails, unwind with a massage at the spa, or book an early tee time on the ranch's eighteen-hole, par-72 golf course.

DAY THREE: *Afternoon*

LUNCH

Check-out isn't until 1:00 P.M., so you can enjoy lunch at the resort's **Country Club Grill** before departing. Your best bet is the Southwestern chicken Caesar salad. It's topped with Feta cheese, toasted pine nuts, and tortilla strips, dressed with a spicy chipolte dressing.

On your way back to San Diego, make a detour to **Shadow Mountain Vineyards** (35124 Highway 79; 760–782–0778). Located on the eastern slopes of Palomar Mountain, the vineyard produces both red and white vintages, which you can sample in their tasting room. Take a moment to relax in the vineyards' garden before heading home.

FOR MORE ROMANCE

With shades of the romantic crime thriller, *The Thomas Crown Affair*, you can take to the skies in a glider at **Warner Springs Sky Sailing** (31930 California Highway 79; 760–782–0404) where their slogan is, "Let your heart soar!" Gliders, or sailplanes, are typically equipped for just one passenger. But at Sky Sailing they accommodate two, so couples can take to the wild blue yonder together for a flight they'll never forget. The sailplanes have cameras mounted to their wings to capture your adventure in the sky. The company offers a number of different flight packages, starting at $78 per couple for a flight around No Name Mountain. Opt for a gentle flight or, if you're an adventurous pair, ask about the thrilling acrobatic ride.

The Road to Nowhere
GOURMET GETAWAY IN DULZURA

UNSPOILED AND UNPRETENTIOUS, DULZURA IS LARGELY IGNORED by tourists. But it has all the ingredients for a fine romantic getaway. Buried deep in the farm and horse country of east San Diego County, just spitting distance from the quiet Mexican border town of Tecate, life moves along at a gentle pace here. The centerpiece of this itinerary is a two-night stay at Brookside Farm Bed & Breakfast Inn, a ten-room refuge nestled amid oak trees by a burbling creek. You can do a lot or you can do a little in sleepy Dulzura, but most folks come to lounge around and do nothing much at all. "We encourage people to just stay around and relax," says Sally Guishard, one of Brookside Farm's hospitable innkeepers. It's a perfect spot to rejuvenate a relationship—and just put your feet up and catch up on some reading. Most couples agree, Brookside Farm is a bit of heaven. We've also thrown in a vintage railroad journey to Tecate, Mexico, that makes this weekend getaway an easy two-nation vacation.

PRACTICAL NOTES: Like anywhere in San Diego's eastern reaches, summers get pretty toasty in Dulzura. If you don't care for the heat, plan this trip for a time from fall through spring, when days are pleasant and clear while nights are crisp and cool. Brookside Farm is delightfully festive during the holidays. Any time of year, bring swimsuits for a dip in the outdoor hot tub. A massage therapist comes to the property on Saturdays, so be sure to schedule a time when making room reservations. If you take the vintage train trip to Tecate, you must bring proof of citizenship (passport, birth certificate, military ID card, or voter registration card will do). Also note that the area code for this itinerary will change to 935 in June 2000.

DAY ONE: *Morning*

Dulzura is a pleasant, forty-minute drive south-east of downtown San Diego. Busy Highway 94 soon gives way to Campo Road and the rolling countryside. In fact, you'll know you're in the country when you pass signs that say RABBITS—these bunnies aren't for sale as pets, but for dinner (look for the sign shaped like a frying pan!).

You can't miss the sign for **Bright Valley Farms** (12310 Campo Road; 619–670–1861 or 888–994–6773) in Spring Valley. These stables are open to the public, and guided, two-hour rides cost $30 per person. Rides typically follow a trail along the Sweetwater River, then through ancient oaks and chaparral for a sweeping hilltop view overlooking the valley below. You guide will tailor the ride to suit your ability. If you're at ease in the saddle, you can lope on the hills.

DAY ONE: *Afternoon*

LUNCH

Entering the tiny hamlet of Dulzura, you'll see the funky, down-home **Dulzura Cafe** (Highway 94; 619–468–9591; inexpensive) on your right. It's definitely worth a stop, if only to soak up little country color.

This cabin-style joint has been around forever, and the menu consists of great old-fashioned burgers, fries, and beer (chichi California cuisine hasn't found its way here just yet). This is a locals' hangout, and if you settle on a regular's barstool, you'll hear about it. They don't really mind—it's just an excuse to strike up a chinwag.

Romance AT A GLANCE

✶ Explore from the saddle on a two-hour, guided horseback tour from **Bright Valley Farms** in Spring Valley (12310 Campo Road; 619–670–1861 or 888–994–6773). The guide will tailor the ride to suit your whims and ability.

✶ Stop for a down-home lunch at the **Dulzura Cafe** (Highway 94; 619–468–9591). Trade gossip and get some tips on area attractions from the friendly locals.

✶ Check into your room at **Brookside Farm Bed & Breakfast Inn** (1373 Marron Valley Road; 619–468–3043). Cool your feet in the creek, visit the menagerie, and pitch a few horseshoes.

✶ Enjoy a four-course dinner prepared by Edd Guishard, Brookside Farm's innkeeper. Edd's gourmet repasts are a highlight of any stay at Brookside Farm.

✶ Spend the day riding a vintage steam train through East County's rugged backcountry to the Mexican border, then pass a few hours exploring the quiet border town of Tecate. The **San Diego Railroad Museum** in Campo (Highway 94 and Sheridan Road; 619–478–9937) organizes Saturday trips.

It's a short drive from the cafe to **Brookside Farm Bed & Breakfast Inn** (1373 Marron Valley Road; 619–468–3043; $85–$120). Since there is a two-night minimum on weekends, ask about the Gourmet Weekend packages ($240–$310). These include accommodations, two country breakfasts, two gourmet dinners, and a cooking class with innkeeper Edd Guishard. Dating back to 1929, the inn was at one time a working dairy farm. Today it offers ten individually decorated rooms. Small and cozy, the rustic Hunter's Cabin is the most popular since it offers the most privacy. It also has a nice screened porch so you can be lulled to sleep by the sound of the rushing stream. But ask about the other rooms, too. La Casita has a country Mexican decor, complete with a gas fireplace, oversize tub, and private courtyard. If your ideal romantic get-away involves staying indoors, reserve the Room with a View (it has a fireplace that opens onto the bedroom and bathroom, plus a refrigerator and private deck) or Jennie's Room, a Victorian fantasy with a gas fireplace, in-room tub, spacious sitting area, and small private porch. In fact, most rooms have a small refrigerator, so you can bring a bottle of your favorite wine. Brookside Farm is decorated throughout with delightful antiques Sally Guishard has collected over the years. But there are no TVs or in-room telephones. You workaholics may suffer from connectivity deprivation, but don't worry, it's good for you.

Once you've settled into your weekend digs, check out the rest of this great property. There's an inviting hot tub with an aviary, as well as a brick terrace shaded by ancient California oak trees and overlooking Dulzura Creek. And feel free to explore Edd and Sally's thriving vegetable and herb garden (you'll sample its fruits later on) and to meet the resident farm animals. Brookside Farm is a true menagerie, with a half-dozen cats, goats, ducks, chickens, a friendly pig, and peacocks that love to show off their stunning plumage.

Really, it is just a wonderful place to hang out, doze on a hammock, and unwind with a bottle of chilled white wine. Only the gentle "thwack" of a badminton racket hitting a shuttlecock or a croquet mallet smacking a ball can break this idyllic quiet. You can play a game, pitch a few horseshoes, or follow the example of most guests and retire for a predinner nap.

DAY ONE: *Evening*

DINNER

Edd and Sally Guishard spent years managing local restaurants before opening the inn in 1983. With that kind of food pedigree, meals are a special event at Brookside Farm. The menu varies, depending on what Edd feels like

Moonlight on the Rails

*If your sweetheart is captivated by the grand, bygone days of rail travel, consider the San Diego Railroad Museum's evening dining service on the **Lunar Limited Dinner Train**. This truly magical event harks back to the age when railroad dining was a wonderful luxury a la the Orient Express. During dinner you're serenaded by a strolling guitarist. Chef Jim Buel, owner and operator of the Burning Tree Restaurant in Boulevard, prepares the meals right on the train in wood-burning ovens, and his menu is based on the classic Union Pacific dining-car menus of yesteryear. On especially balmy nights the engineer stops the train so passengers can get off and walk along or dance beside the train in the moonlight. Reservations are recommended, as the Lunar Limited has a capacity of twenty-six passengers (call ahead for the year's scheduled runs). Evening dinner train rides are $75 per person; call (619) 535-3030 for reservations.*

preparing. Since much of the produce is grown on the farm, you can expect seasonal dishes—maybe chicken breasts in peanut sauce with couscous and fresh peas, followed by lemon pie. And because you don't have to drive anywhere after dinner, you can indulge in some wine with your meal.

Meals are a communal affair, so guests usually get pretty chummy over dinner, and the evening inevitably turns to board games or card games in the lounge. Coffee and after-dinner drinks keep the good times rolling.

DAY TWO: *Morning*

BREAKFAST

Ah, the smell of fresh-baked breads and rolls is enough to lure anyone out of bed. Like dinner the night before, breakfast is all made fresh on the premises. Homemade jams and jellies provide the perfect companions for Edd's baked goods, and he also whips up a hot egg dish. He makes his own sausage as well.

With the perfect weather it's fun just to find a hammock and enjoy the shade of the trees. However, you'll find it worth your while to spend the day traveling back in time. Hop in the car and continue southeast on Highway 94 to the tiny town of Campo and the **San Diego Railroad Museum** (Highway 94 and Sheridan Road; 619–478–9937; Campo-Tecate train journeys are $35 per person). This isn't just some musty museum. On the contrary, you're going

to take a trip on an authentic Wild West steam train south to Tecate, Mexico (this excursion is only available Saturdays). The train departs promptly at 10:00 A.M. and chugs over trestle bridges, through tunnels, and amid the rocky, dramatic backcountry (you half expect Jesse James to come riding 'round a boulder to rob the train). It's a pretty leisurely journey and takes about an hour to cover the 15 miles to Tecate.

DAY TWO: *Afternoon*

Once you reach the border, you'll transfer to a bus for the short ride into Tecate. You'll have several hours to explore this small, friendly border city. Unlike bustling, chaotic Tijuana to the west, Tecate is a hardworking, blue-collar town. Upon arriving, you can join the group for an hour-long tour and tasting at the **Tecate Brewery** (it's included in your train ticket); brews crafted here are sold in more than one hundred countries. Or you can strike out on your own to browse through some of the small shops and galleries that sell local crafts and artwork. Much of the town's activity revolves around the central park.

LUNCH

You can choose some nibbles from street vendors to share on a bench under the trees, or sit down for a lunch of tacos, quesadillas, or enchiladas at one of the outdoor tables at **El Jardin** (inexpensive), which is on the park. If you need a sweet fix after lunch, amble over to **El Mejor Pan**, a bakery on Avendia Benito Juarez a block northeast of the park. And don't bother to exchange currency—U.S. dollars are readily accepted in this savvy border community.

The train departs from Tecate promptly at 2:30 P.M. On the journey back, the glorious effects of good food, beer, and afternoon sun will conspire with the gentle rocking of the train to send you into a blissful sleep.

After your day on the rails, you'll return to Brookside Farm by late afternoon. If you planned ahead, you've already scheduled time with the masseuse who visits on Saturdays. If not, you can always soak in the hot tub under the grape arbor.

DINNER

Once again you'll have dinner in the farmhouse, where you can exchange tales of your railroad adventure with the other guests. What's on the menu

tonight? Maybe shrimp in cilantro and garlic sauce, or game hens in plum sauce, followed by fresh peach pie or chocolate zucchini cake.

Since this is your last night at Brookside Farm, you may choose to retire early to the cozy confines of your room or enjoy another soak in the hot tub.

DAY THREE: *Morning*

BREAKFAST

Wrap up your stay with a leisurely breakfast, again prepared compliments of Edd. If you're very nice, he may even share a recipe or two.

Not quite ready to return to the real world? After leaving Brookside farm, head north from Dulzura to Barrett Lake. There you can rent a boat and fishing poles to spend a few hours drifting on the lake with the sun reflecting off the calm water. One end of the lake is dammed (the Barrett Dam being one of the larger dams built in the 1920s) and something of an impressive sight. If neither of you hooks a fish, the local **Barrett Café** (Highway 94 at Barrett Lake Road; 619–468–3416; inexpensive) serves fresh fish caught from the lake, with its famous fish fry and all-you-can-eat menu.

FOR MORE ROMANCE

OK, so dropping a line into a lake isn't thrilling enough. Brookside Farm is just moments away from **Parachutes over San Diego** (13531 Otay Lakes Road; 800–707–5867; $155–$195 per person), where you can sit and watch the skydivers do their thing. Couples in search of more "T" factor can sign up for a skydiving class, doing static line or free fall on a tandem jump from 14,000 feet. This is a full day's excursion, but on a clear day there is nothing more exhilarating. However, it's certainly not for the faint of heart.

Mile-High Idyll
An Escape to Idyllwild

S OUTHERN CALIFORNIA ISN'T ALL BEACHES AND DESERTS. In a short, two-hour drive you can escape the urban sprawl and emerge in a pristine, mile-high mountain retreat. Idyllwild is a quaint alpine hamlet with authentic log-cabin hideaways, Victorian inns, and deluxe B&Bs. It's also a year-round destination with wintertime snow and summertime hiking. Nestled in the shadow of Mount San Jacinto and the Santa Rosa Mountains, Idyllwild has an inviting rustic elegance. It's home to Idyllwild Arts (a boarding school for teens) and an annual celebrity film festival every October, so it's a crossroads where the arts crowd mingles with outdoorsy types who come to hike, rock-climb, horseback ride, and mountain bike on a network of more than 275 miles of high-altitude trails. With well-stocked bookstores, fine-dining restaurants, and bustling coffeehouses, this compact town has a welcome sophistication with a dash of down-home friendliness. This weekend itinerary encourages you to rough it a little on the trails by day, then spoil yourselves with well-earned gourmet meals at night.

PRACTICAL NOTES: Plan an early getaway—no later than 2:00 P.M.—to avoid the nerve-wracking Friday-afternoon crush on Interstate 15. This itinerary highlights the terrific hiking in Idyllwild, so it's best done in spring, summer, or fall. You may still be able to get in some hiking in winter, depending on how much snow the area gets. Whenever you go, you'll need to pick up a $5.00 Adventure Pass parking permit, as well as a free day-use permit for hiking; both are available at the ranger station in town. We've recommended two places to stay, but there are dozens of

Romance

AT A GLANCE

✷ *Make reservations at*
Creekstone Inn Bed & Breakfast
(54950 Pine Crest Avenue; 909–659–
3342 or 800–409–2127), an upscale
B&B just steps from town, or rent a cozy
*cottage at **Fern Valley Inn** (25240 Fern*
Valley Road; 909–659–2205).

✷ *Browse through the shops in town. Pick*
up a few gourmet goodies and wine at the
***Epicurean** (54791 North Circle Drive; 909–*
659–5251 or 800–659–0008) to take back
to your room, or find hiking maps and gear
*at **Nomad Ventures Mountain Equipage***
(54415 North Circle Drive; 909–659–4853).

✷ *Have an elegant dinner by the fire at*
***Restaurant Gastrognome** (54381 Ridgeview;*
909–659–5055).

✷ *Fuel up for a day on the trails with a bowl*
*of oatmeal at **Oma's European Bakery and***
***Restaurant** (54360 North Circle Drive; 909–*
*659–2979). Then walk over to the **Fairway***
***Supermarket** (54111 Village Center Drive;*
909–659–2737) to collect water and picnic
supplies.

✷ *Spend the day trekking up **Devil's***
***Slide Trail**, or just explore the easy*
***Ernie Maxwell Scenic Trail**. Or take a*
*guided horseback ride at **"Hay Dude"***
***Ranch** (McCall County Park Mountain*
Center; 909–763–2473).

✷ *Settle into a candlelit booth*
*for dinner at **Antonelli's***
Seafood Ristorante
(26345 Highway 243;
909–659– 5500).

cabins, inns and B&Bs in the area. A call to the **Associated Idyllwild Rentals** (909–659–5520) will get you rates and availability. Remember, most cabins and inns have a two-night minimum stay on weekends and holidays.

DAY ONE: *Afternoon*

Assuming you leave San Diego by early afternoon, you'll arrive in Idyllwild in the middle or late afternoon. Either way, you'll be right on time to check into **Creekstone Inn Bed & Breakfast** (54950 Pine Crest Avenue; 909–659–3342 or 800–409–2127; $95–$145). The nine-room inn started out as a soda fountain in 1942 but was refurbished in 1994 as a luxury B&B in a cozy, upscale country motif. Spoil your sweetheart and reserve one of the three rooms with a fireplace and whirlpool tub for two (you'll be glad to have it after a day of hiking).

Traveling on a tighter budget? Rent a darling cottage at **Fern Valley Inn** (25240 Fern Valley Road; 909–659–2205; $70–$110), two miles north of town. For ample privacy request one of the individual cottages. The Loft is an A-frame cabin with a fireplace, full kitchen, and queen bed tucked in a cozy loft.

After settling into your digs, amble into town for the rest of the afternoon to check out the shops. Walking down North Circle Drive toward the center of town, you'll pass several shops worth a stop. If your honey has a sweet tooth, go into **The Costermonger** (54750 North Circle; 909–659–2151), which

sells products from the British Isles. Authentic wool caps, scarves, and sweaters are on sale there, but the real treat is an impressive selection of British candy and cookies (sorry, *biscuits*)—Aero Bars, Wispa Bars, and the great British Mars Bar (similar to, but better than, their American cousin). Just up the road **Stonehill Books** (54425 North Circle Drive; 909–659–9882) stocks bestsellers and other reads. In this dog-friendly town, the locals often browse the stacks with their pooches in tow. If you need any hiking gear or want to pick up a good trail map, stop by **Nomad Ventures Mountain Equipage** (54415 North Circle Drive; 909–659–4853).

At the bottom of North Circle Drive, you'll come to the town's busy main intersection with the Banning-Idyllwild Highway (Highway 243). At the center of the junction is the **Fort**, a modern-day wood fort that houses a variety of shops catering to the tourist trade. You'll find stores that sell shoes, country apparel, arts and crafts, apple pies, and the like. Across the road is the quaint **Village Lane** (54200 North Circle Drive). A tiny entrance leads to a narrow alley of more unusual boutiques, including **Wooley's** (909–659–0017), which sells cuddly sheepskin hats, gloves, and scarves. Nights can be chilly here, so you may want to pick up a little something to keep your sweetheart warm and toasty!

Be sure to stop at the **Idyllwild Ranger Station** (Pine Crest Avenue at Highway 243; 909–659–2117) to pick up two items you'll need for tomorrow's hike. The first is a free Wilderness Permit. The second is a $5.00 Adventure Pass, which is mandatory to park near tomorrow's trail-head at **Humber Park**. If you plan to take the all-day hike to the **Upper Palm Springs Aerial Tramway**, you'll also need to request a permit to hike on **Devil's Slide Trail**.

On your way back to the inn, stop by the **Epicurean** (54791 North Circle Drive; 909–659–5251 or 800–659–0008). Billing itself as "Idyllwild's most romantic setting," the Epicurean features a cluster of separate lodges housing gift, apparel, and gourmet food shops amid pleasant gardens. Pop into one of the charcuteries to pick up a bottle of wine and some cheese to enjoy by the fire in your room.

DAY ONE: *Evening*

DINNER

Seafood, Chinese, Mexican, Italian, all-American fare—Idyllwild certainly doesn't lack for fine places to eat. Tonight make reservations for a fire-

side table at **Restaurant Gastrognome** (54381 Ridgeview; 909-659-5055; moderate to expensive). The menu offers a nice mix of fresh seafood, steak, lamb, pasta, and salads (with optional "light eater's" portions). After dinner relax in the bar with a cocktail or an Irish coffee. For more casual Mexican fare, try **La Casita** (54650 North Circle Drive; 909-659-3038; inexpensive to moderate).

To make it proper date night, find out what's playing at the **Rustic Theatre** (54290 North Circle Drive; 909-659-2747). This one-screen theater is a delightful throwback to another time—the modest concession stand leads to a high-beamed, cavernous theater showing first-run movies.

After the movie stroll hand-in-hand back to the inn under a sparkling canopy of stars. Idyllwild's altitude and clean air makes them seem close enough to touch. If it's chilly you can always warm up by the fire in your room.

DAY TWO: *Morning*

BREAKFAST

A terrific spot for breakfast is **Oma's European Bakery and Restaurant** (54360 North Circle Drive; 909-659-2979; inexpensive). Sit by the stone fireplace inside, or relax under the pine trees at a table draped in a pink tablecloth. Fresh-baked pastries and bread with a Dutch influence make for a special start to the day. To fuel up for today's hike, maybe order a hearty bowl of oatmeal accompanied by raisins and brown sugar.

Following an early breakfast, walk over to the **Fairway Supermarket** (54111 Village Center Drive; 909-659-2737) to stock up on picnic supplies and plenty of water. What today's itinerary includes depends on how hardy you feel. Idyllwild's backcountry offers some of the best high-altitude hiking in Southern California, and you can spend the entire day hiking through the Mount San Jacinto State Wilderness.

There are more than 275 miles of trails to explore in the Idyllwild forest. For a full day's adventure, drive to **Humber Park** (at the end of Fern Valley Road), park and follow **Devil's Slide Trail** and **Willow Creek Trail** to **Long Valley** and the **Upper Palm Springs Aerial Tramway**. This is an all-day journey at 8,000 feet-plus and the air gets a bit thin up here, so allow plenty of time to hike at an easy pace. You won't want to rush through this primeval forest of lodgepole, sugar, and sweet-scented Jeffrey pines. Plenty of spots along the way will beckon you to stop, sip some water, and just sit back to listen to the wind rustle through the trees. Depending on your pace it will take about

hours to reach the Aerial Tramway. The expansive observation deck overlooking Palm Springs and the desert floor below is a smashing place for a picnic.

If you don't want to spend all day on the trail, take the more modest, but no less beautiful, **Ernie Maxwell Scenic Trail**, a 2.6-mile path ideal for novice hikers. Beginning in Humber Park, the trail is a popular route with local joggers, walkers, and equestrians. It's also a terrific introduction to the area—you'll see Little Taquitz Creek, Marion Mountain, and Suicide Rock.

Another way to explore Idyllwild's backcountry is from the saddle. **"Hay Dude" Ranch** (McCall County Park Mountain Center; 909–763–2473), located about ten minutes outside of Idyllwild, offers one- and two-hour guided trail rides ($25 an hour with a two-horse minimum; make reservations at least twenty-four hours in advance). The ranch has several packages, including picnic rides, sunset rides, and even overnight pack trips.

DAY TWO: *Evening*

When you get back to town from your day hiking or horseback riding, you've earned a pleasant rest before dinner. At Creekstone Inn relax in the giant whirlpool in your room, maybe with a glass of wine. Staying at Fern Valley Inn? Take a long, hot shower and unwind by the fire.

DINNER

Antonelli's Seafood Ristorante, located just on the outskirts of town (26345 Highway 243; 909–659–5500; expensive), is a small country-style *cucina* serving Italian cuisine with an emphasis on fresh seafood. Reserve one of the intimate booths and savor ahi, salmon, or halibut by candlelight. And because you've worked so hard on hiking trails today, you can indulge a little. Ask to see their wonderful dessert tray, which includes their sinful Death by Chocolate. What a way to go. . . .

DAY THREE: *Morning*

BREAKFAST

You're in no hurry today, so sleep in and linger over breakfast. A full gourmet breakfast is served at 9:00 A.M. in the sun room of the Creekstone

Inn. If you're staying at Fern Valley Inn, one of you can pop into town to pick up hot coffee and freshly baked scones at **Uptown Cafe** (54750 North Circle Drive; 909–659–5212; inexpensive). Or the two of you can venture out to the **Idyllwild Cafe** (26600 Highway 243; 909–659–2210; inexpensive) for a hearty country breakfast of scrambled eggs, sausage, and giant biscuits.

Pass the rest of the morning doing, well, pretty much nothing. Read by the fire, stroll through town, or just sit outside and soak up the mountain sunshine before a late-morning checkout. On your way out of town, stop at **Country Farms** (25980 Highway 243; 909–659–3434) to pick up wine, cheese, gourmet olives, fruit, and whatever else tempts you for a picnic on the way home.

For More Romance

Once you've hiked up to the Mountain Station of the **Palm Springs Aerial Tramway**, (888–515–8726), you may have time for a ride on the tram ($17.65 round-trip). It's a fourteen-minute descent down to the desert floor with an astounding elevation change of 5,873 feet. As the tram passes through different altitudes, you'll see plant life similar to what you'd see from Alaska to Mexico's Sonoran Desert. Not up for that kind of thrill? Amble over to the Lone Valley stables, located just behind the tram's mountain station, to saddle up for a twenty-minute, guided mule ride through the pines. Rides are just $7.00 per person; no reservations needed.

Desert Blossoms
SPRING IN ANZA-BORREGO DESERT STATE PARK

HEN MOST PEOPLE THINK OF SAN DIEGO, beachy *Baywatch* images leap to mind. But the area reveals another face in the pristine desert preserve known as **Anza-Borrego Desert State Park**. With more than 600,000 acres, it's the largest state park in the nation, yet for years it remained a Southern California secret. But word has gotten out since national publications started spotlighting this unspoiled gem. While the park is welcoming more visitors than ever, there still isn't much more than miles of country road winding through the enormous desert valley. The tiny town of **Borrego Springs** is the oasis in the midst of the badlands and canyons. It's an unpretentious outpost that's a far cry from Palm Springs, its glitzier cousin to the north. But you'll find plenty of civilized touches, including a sweet B&B or an elegant resort to stay the night. This itinerary catches Anza-Borrego at its showiest during the spring wildflower season, but it's a wonderful retreat in fall and winter, too.

PRACTICAL NOTES: Spring is prime time in Borrego, when delicate wildflowers carpet the desert floor in hues of pink, purple, yellow, and white. It's also the park's busiest season, so make reservations well in advance. And consider a midweek getaway, since daytrippers flood the park's most popular trails on weekends. As with any desert getaway, you'll need hats, sunglasses, and plenty of high-SPF sunscreen. A light jacket helps ward off the chill of spring mornings and evenings. Expect pleasant daytime temperatures in the high 70°s and low 80°s; at night the mercury dips to the low 50°s. If you want to explore the park's remotest reaches, better rent a four-wheel-drive vehicle. Trust us, you do not want to get stuck out here.

Romance
AT A GLANCE

* Stay at **Borrego Valley Inn** (405 Palm Canyon Drive; 760-767-0311) or **La Casa del Zorro Desert Resort** (3845 Yaqui Pass Road; 760-767-5983 or 800-824-1884). Whichever you choose, request a room with a fireplace to chase away the evening chill.

* Check out the wonderful display of wildflowers and palm trees along the **Borrego Palm Canyon Nature Trail.** Don't forget to dip your feet in a cool stream. It's an easy 3 miles round-trip.

* Dine by the fireplace at La Casa del Zorro's elegant restaurant.

* Wrap up the evening with a cocktail under the stars. Maybe soak in the Jacuzzi before bed.

* Get up early to watch the sun rise over the Santa Rosa Mountains.

* Stock up on picnic supplies and rent mountain bikes from **Carrizo Bikes** (648 Palm Canyon Drive; 760-767-3872) to explore other trails in the park.

For information about **Anza-Borrego Desert State Park,** call (760) 767-5311. Check on the status of the flowers with the spring wildflower hot line, (760) 767-4684. The **Borrego Springs Chamber of Commerce** (800-559-5524; www.borregosprings.org) will mail you comprehensive information about lodging, dining, and attractions. If you want to plan a desert-mountain escape, combine this with Itinerary 13 to Julian. Both communities show off San Diego's down-home, backcountry side.

DAY ONE: *Morning*

Borrego is 90 miles east of downtown San Diego, and much of that is on two-lane country roads. Hit the highway sometime after breakfast and allow about two hours for the trip. There are several routes you can take. The most popular follows Highway 78 through Ramona and Julian before hooking up with County Road S3 into Borrego. Along the way you can stop for coffee and freshly baked donuts at **Dudley's Bakery** (Highway 78 and 79; 760-765-0488; inexpensive) in Santa Ysabel.

Just opened in 1998 **Borrego Valley Inn** (405 Palm Canyon Drive; 760-767-0311; www.borregovalleyinn.com; $80-$145) is an appropriate touch of Santa Fe in the Southern California desert. Most of the inn's fourteen rooms, housed in a series of low-slung adobe buildings, have fireplaces, kitchenettes, and private patios. They're decorated in casual, Southwest style—rough-hewn furnishings and bright Mexican blankets—and make for a cozy retreat.

If you want to stretch the budget, book a private casita at the seventy-seven-room **La Casa del Zorro Desert Resort** (3845 Yaqui Pass Road;

760–767–5323 or 800–824–1884; www.lacasadelzorro.com; $85–$345). Some have private pools; others have baby grand pianos in case you're inspired to serenade your sweetheart. Even the regular guest rooms are pleasantly spacious, and most have fireplaces, too. The decor here is elegant Old California with wood-beam ceilings and recently redone rooms. Facilities at the resort include a fully outfitted gym and a terrific, six-court tennis complex. Courts are lighted for night play if you feel like lobbing a few under the stars.

DAY ONE: *Afternoon*

LUNCH

Located on Borrego Springs's main drag, **Carlee's Place** (660 Palm Canyon Drive; 760–767–3522; inexpensive) is a friendly local hangout with a delightfully trippy decor. Stepping in from the bright sun, it takes a moment for your eyes to adjust to this dark den. It's done from floor to ceiling in royal blue, which gives it an oddly underwater ambience. Locals gather at the bar every afternoon, but you can settle into a blue booth for privacy. The menu runs mostly to burgers and fries, washed down with beer on tap. From Carlee's it's a short stroll to **Borrego Valley Foods** (Palm Canyon Drive at Christmas Circle; 760–767–5321) to pick up plenty of water for this afternoon's hike.

After lunch drive to Anza-Borrego Desert State Park's **Visitors Center** (200 Palm Canyon Drive; 760–767–4205) to start your desert exploration. The center is a hub of activity where rangers post a list of wildflowers in bloom and a log of peninsular bighorn sheep sightings. Pick up a trail map from the rangers, as well as the *Wildflowers of Anza-Borrego Desert State Park* brochure to help you identify the many delicate blossoms. Another smart buy is the *Weekender's Guide*, a beautifully photographed guide to hiking trails throughout the park.

But you won't have to venture far to find one of the best. **Borrego Palm Canyon Nature Trail** starts just past the campground and gently climbs a mile and half to a lush oasis of California fan palms. No need to rush, though, because if the winter rain cooperated, you'll enjoy a dazzling springtime floral display. This time of year even the cacti bloom and you'll see squat barrel cacti wearing a crown of yellow blossoms or flat prickly pear cacti adorned with showy lemon-hued petals. Daisylike desert stars and magenta sand verbena spread delicate, lacy

Spot a Borrego

Anza-Borrego takes its name from the park's most treasured and threatened resident, the peninsular bighorn sheep. Dubbed the "borrego cimarron" by early Spanish explorers, these sheep once roamed through much of North America. Today there are fewer than 300, and most of them live in this park. In fact, the park was established in 1933 in part to provide a haven for these endangered animals. While they enjoy protected status, the harsh environment still takes a toll. Only about a quarter of newborn lambs survive their first year. Many fall prey to the summer heat, which climbs to 120 degrees, or to hungry mountain lions and coyotes on the prowl.

Naturally, seeing a bighorn sheep is a rare treat. With their massive, curling horns and long faces, they boast the sleek elegance of an Egyptian pharaoh. But it takes a patient eye to spot them. They're right at home among the rocks, and their tawny coats blend into the sandy desert landscape. You may be lucky enough to spy a ewe and her lamb tucked in the craggy hillside. One of the best places to spot them is along the Borrego Palm Canyon Nature Trail. If you glimpse a ram sipping from the stream and nibbling on a jojoba plant, count your trip a success!

carpets across the sand. Even the tall, spindly ocotillo bush wears red flowers like a fresh manicure at the tips of its 8-foot stems. You'll find this route is a treat for all the senses. If it's rained recently, you'll smell the smoky scent of the creosote bush. Also stop to rub a few white petals of desert lavender bush between your fingers and release a heady aroma that's sure to remind you of Provence. At the end of the trail, kick off your shoes and cool your feet in the palm grove's inviting pools and waterfalls.

You can hike back the way you came or follow an alternate route that loops through the valley back to the campground parking area. Either way you may spot some of the park's elusive residents—perhaps a roadrunner skittering across the trail, or a coyote loping in the distance, or even a rare peninsular bighorn sheep—a member of the small flock that roams throughout the park.

Still have energy to spare? The half-mile Panoramic Overlook Trail, departing from the campground, is short and steep. But after climbing to the top of a ridge, you'll be rewarded with a sweeping view of the Borrego Valley. If you've had enough, head back to your hotel to cool off with a dip in the pool. Splash around, then claim a pair of

lounge chairs so you can sit back and watch the sun sink behind Vallecito Mountains.

DAY ONE: *Evening*

Dress up a bit (casually elegant is just fine—jackets required for gents) for an evening at the restaurant of **La Casa del Zorro** (expensive). Start with a cocktail in **Fox Den**, the resort's cozy, firelit lounge and piano bar.

DINNER

Reservations are a must this time of year (it's not a bad idea to book a table when you make room reservations), especially if you want to dine at a romantic fireside table in the dining room of La Casa del Zorro. The room is spacious, yet a warmly elegant Southwestern ambience with Western-cowboy artworks gives it an intimate feel. A recently revamped menu features Continental favorites with a contemporary California spin.

Without lights blocking the view, you can count on a terrific star show in the desert. Sit out by the pool, share a champagne toast, and scan the skies for shooting stars. Don't forget to make a wish! If it's a balmy evening, you may even want to take a late-night dip.

DAY TWO: *Morning*

Request an early-morning wake-up call so you can catch the sunrise over the 9,000-foot Santa Rosa Mountains. Dawn in the desert is a special treat as the sun gradually warms the rocks and sand to fiery shades of gold and paints the surrounding mountains to hues of purple and blue. If you're not early risers by habit, you can always snuggle back into bed.

BREAKFAST

Continental breakfast is served in the casual dining room at the Borrego Springs Inn, but one of you may want to fetch a few goodies to bring back to the room. At La Casa del Zorro, room service will happily deliver breakfast to your door. Ask them to set it up on your patio or balcony.

After breakfast check out and drive into town and make another pit stop at Borrego Valley Foods to stock up on picnic supplies and more

water for the day. While you're in town, rent mountain bikes from **Carrizo Bikes** (648 Palm Canyon Drive; 760–767–3872). Rates are $7.00 for the first hour and $5.00 for each additional hour. If you plan to spend all day on the trails, opt for the $29.00, twenty-four-hour rate. Owner Dan Cain will outfit you with helmets and happily recommend some good routes. Your options range from little-used paved roads and gentle dirt paths to gnarly, teeth-rattling trails.

If you don't mind climbing a bit (and isn't that what a mountain bike's low gears are for?), depart from the Visitors Center along the **California Riding and Hiking Trail**. This climbs about 5 miles to an overlook that offers views of **Hellhole Canyon**. Feeling ambitious? Continue on this trail to where it crosses the S22 road and hooks up with the **Jasper Trail**, a dirt road that gently descends 1,000 feet over 7 miles. Continue through **Grapevine Canyon** to hook up with the main road and loop back to town and the Visitors Center.

For More Romance

Want to lie on the beach in the middle of the desert? Plan an excursion to the **Salton Sea State Recreation Area**, less than forty minutes' drive from Borrego Springs. As you drop deeper into the valley, the Salton Sea spreads before you like a weird and wonderful mirage 220 feet below sea level. It's the largest lake in California, covering more than 360 square miles and offering more than 110 miles of shoreline. It's a popular spot with campers, anglers, and boaters, but especially bird-watchers. More than four million birds flock to the Salton Sea every winter.

Romance among the Rocks

Joshua Tree National Park

The cities aflood / And our love turns to rust / We're beaten and blown by the wind / Trampled in dust. / I'll show you a place / High on a desert plain / Where the streets have no name. . . . — **U2, *The Joshua Tree***

DON'T HAVE A BIG BUDGET, BUT REALLY NEED A GETAWAY FOR TWO? Joshua Tree National Park is about two and a half hours from San Diego and feels like another planet with its otherworldly landscape of Joshua trees and massive boulders. This itinerary encourages you to explore the park by day—clamber over its famous rocks, explore its oases, and spot the abundant wildlife (including real-life roadrunners and Wyle E. Coyotes)—and kick back at night to admire the stars and maybe catch a flick at the local drive-in. Keep your spending in check at one of the area's affordable inns while you enjoy a welcome measure of cozy comfort and ample privacy.

PRACTICAL NOTES: Summers are hot, which makes October through April the best time to visit. Daytime temperatures are in the 60°s and 70°s—perfect for hiking. In winter, lows drop into the 30°s and may even bring a dusting of snow, so bring a jacket and gloves for chilly mornings and evenings. Light hiking boots are fine for trekking along sandy trails and scrambling over boulders. Be sure to pack high-SPF sunscreen, hats, and sunglasses. Also bring a day pack to tote water on the trail, as well as a cool-

Romance

AT A GLANCE

✻ Stay at one of the area's small inns or B&Bs, such as **29 Palms Inn** (73950 Twentynine Palms Highway; 760-367-3505) or **Joshua Tree Inn Bed & Breakfast** (61259 Twentynine Palms Highway; 760-366-1188 or 800-366-1444).

✻ Check out the local art scene at **29 Palms Artists' Guild Art Gallery and Gift Shop** (74055 Cottonwood Drive; 760-367-7819).

✻ Enjoy a gourmet dinner under the stars at 29 Palms Inn. You may glimpse the resident barn owls flitting among the palm trees.

✻ Catch a double feature at **Smith's Ranch Drive-In** (4584 Adobe Road; 760-367-7713).

✻ Use you second day to scramble over the boulders and explore remote oases in **Joshua Tree National Park.**

✻ Catch a performance at the **Hi-Desert Playhouse** (61231 Twentynine Palms Highway; 760-366-3777) or take your sweetheart two-steppin' at **Pappy & Harriet's Palace** (53688 Pioneertown Road; 760-365-5956) in Pioneertown.

✻ On your way home unwind in the mineral pools at the **Desert Springs Spa Hotel** (10805 Palm Drive; 760-329-7000 or 800-808-7727).

er to stash snacks and cold drinks in the car. A couple of camp chairs are a nice touch so you can relax after a picnic lunch and enjoy the view. For more information about Joshua Tree National Park, call (760) 367-7511, check out the National Park Service web page at www.nps.gov/jotr/home.html, or call the privately run Park Center, (760) 366-3448. You can combine this trip with Itinerary 22 to Temecula's wine country—it's on the way to Joshua Tree.

DAY ONE: *Morning*

After breakfast at home, make a mid-morning exit. From San Diego, take Interstate 15 north to Interstate 10. Then drive east to Highway 62, which turns into Twentynine Palms Highway and drops you into Joshua Tree National Park. You may want to stop in Temecula on the way to check out antiques stores in Old Town Temecula or sample the vintages at a couple of local wineries (see Itinerary 22). The trip to Joshua Tree takes about two and a half hours without stops, but it's a scenic trip as you pass through the rocky terrain of North San Diego County, with its acres of avocado groves, and then drive through small towns and bedroom communities toward the vast, open spaces of the high desert. One of the oddest sights on your route will be the Wind Farm, a veritable forest of towering electric windmills that look like something the artist Cristo would create. Instead the windmills cleverly harness the breeze to generate electricity for the desert communities. **EV Adventures** leads ninety-minute tours ($23 per person) four times daily; call (760) 251-1997 for reservations.

DAY ONE: *Afternoon*

LUNCH

You'll be ready for a bite to eat and a cold brew by the time you reach the environs of Joshua Tree. In Yucca Valley, cool and cavernous **Water Canyon** (55844 Twentynine Palms Highway; 760–365–7771; inexpensive) is a coffeehouse that serves a light menu of salads and wraps. Cool off with an iced coffee drink or a bottle of imported beer. In Joshua Tree, **Jeremy's Cybercafe & Beer Haus** (61597 Twentynine Palms Highway; 760–366–9799; inexpensive) serves sandwiches, veggie burgers, and tasty microbrews on tap. If you must check your e-mail, this is the place to do it.

Accommodations in the communities along Twentynine Palms Highway—Yucca Valley, Joshua Tree, and Twentynine Palms—are affordable, low-key inns, B&Bs, and motels. You can't miss the roadside **Joshua Tree Inn Bed & Breakfast** (61259 Twentynine Palms Highway; 760–366–1188 or 800–366–1444; $75–$150) in the hamlet of Joshua Tree. Built in the 1930s, it has quite a history. The Rolling Stones have stayed here; so has the cast of TV's *Saturday Night Live*. Folk rocker Gram Parsons died of a drug overdose in 1973 in the oft-requested Room 8. But don't expect a rock-group roadie's dive. Current owner Evelyn Shirbroun has bestowed a rustic elegance on the inn's ten rooms. Some have cool terra-cotta floors and ceiling fans; others boast cheerful Mexican tiles in the bathroom. Breakfast is served in the lodge dining room, where dinner is also served on Friday and Saturday evenings. A crackling fire in the stone fireplace chases away the chill on winter evenings. When making reservations, ask about packages including breakfast, a boxed lunch, and dinner.

In the area's main hub, Twentynine Palms, **29 Palms Inn** (73950 Inn Avenue; 760–367–3505; www.29palmsinn.com; $65–$260) sits on the edge of the national park's Oasis of Mara pond. Individually decorated rooms are in small adobe cottages and old frame cabins (they've been in the family since 1929) scattered over 70 acres. Most have private patios, and some have fireplaces. The inn is definitely a lounge and do-nothing kind of place with hammocks, a fine poolside bar, and a restaurant.

After checking in, cool off with a dip in the pool or check out the area's thriving art scene. The eerie landscape is a magnet for artists who are inspired by the play of light and shadow on the rocks, trees, and cacti. In fact, the town of Twentynine Palms proudly calls itself "An Oasis of

Murals." A dozen murals adorn buildings in the downtown area and document the area's colorful history, from early gold miners to modern-day marines. (Twentynine Palms seems to have a tattoo parlor on every block to accommodate the local soldiers' artistic needs.) Catch local exhibits at the **29 Palms Artists' Guild Art Gallery and Gift Shop** (74055 Cottonwood Drive; 760–367–7819) and **Desert Iron Gallery** (6455 Mesquite; 760–367–5257).

DAY ONE: *Evening*

DINNER

Even if you don't stay at **29 Palms Inn**, do plan to have dinner there (moderate). It's an ideal spot to rub elbows with the locals and swap travel tips with other road warriors while feasting on steak, rosemary chicken, shrimp scampi, or pasta. You can eat indoors beside a bar lit up with festive chili-pepper lights, but the poolside tables are more popular—and more romantic. For more privacy, request a corner table. It's an ideal spot to linger under the stars and watch barn owls flit among the palm trees. Don't be surprised if the resident six-toed cat sidles up for a handout.

 When was the last time you went to a drive-in theater? After dinner catch the second half of a first-run double feature at **Smith's Ranch Drive-In** (4584 Adobe Road; 760–367–7713). Admission is $3 per person. Load up on goodies from the concession stand, tune in the sound on your car radio, and sit back to enjoy the show. If what's on the screen doesn't thrill you, the stars overhead will. You'll spot Venus, the Milky Way, and maybe even a shooting star or a passing satellite. Or slide into the back seat to make out. Isn't that what drive-ins are for?

DAY TWO: *Morning*

BREAKFAST

Have breakfast on the patio at your inn, or flip a coin to decide which one of you will bring back coffee and pastries to enjoy in your room.

Ask your innkeeper to prepare a boxed lunch, if possible, to enjoy during your leisurely day in the park. Otherwise, stop at a local grocery store to stock up on picnic supplies and plenty of bottled water, since there are few potable sources within the park. Park rangers recommend at least one gallon per person per day. You can load up on goodies, including homemade fudge, at the **Finicky Coyote** (73511 Twentynine Palms Highway; 760–367–2429).

Enter **Joshua Tree National Park** (760–367–7511) through the north entrance at Twentynine Palms. The entrance fee is $10 per car, and it's valid for seven consecutive days. Follow the two-lane main road as it winds along the desert floor for about 10 miles and park near the sign for Skull Rock. From here you can follow a well-marked trail through the massive boulders precariously stacked atop each other like a giant's building blocks. Gazing up, you'll likely spot a climber or two scaling the face of Skull Rock. This trail is an easy 1.7-mile loop that takes you through the Jumbo Rocks campground. Hop back in the car and continue along the main road another 10 miles or so to the Barker Dam Trail, a flat, 1-mile loop that takes in two interesting sights. First, you can't miss the water-filled dam, built by early ranchers to collect water for cattle. Then follow the trail and signs to the Indian petroglyphs. There's a sad story attached to them, however. The petroglyphs were carved into the rocks by Indians long ago. Unfortunately a film crew saw fit to paint over some of these carvings to make them more visible, and that's what you see from the trail. But you can scramble up onto the rocks to see some of the petroglyphs in their original state.

Come to the Promised Land

If God had put Dr. Seuss in charge of botany design, he would have created the Joshua tree. Nature's oddball looks like a cross between a palm tree and a cactus. It's really an overgrown yucca plant with furry-looking bark and spiky tufts of fronds at the end of twisting branches. The tree was named by weary Mormon pioneers on a long trek across the Mojave desert—its outstretched branches reminded them of the prophet Joshua welcoming them to the promised land. No one knows how old these otherworldly plants are, though the oldest in the park is estimated to be a ripe old 900. In spring, ivory blossoms grace the branches.

Go Climb a Rock

Massive boulders and sheer cliffs attract thousands of rock climbers to Joshua Tree National Park—there are more than 4,500 established climbing routes. You'll probably glimpse climbers slowly scaling the sheer rocks like real-life Spidermen. If you want to join them, contact one of the many outfitters in the area. Two are Joshua Tree Rock Climbing School (760-366-4745 or 800-890-4745) and Nomad Adventures (760-366-4684). Both offer daylong classes for beginners (starting at $75 per person), as well as private guide services ($110–$120 per person per day). They'll provide all your gear—helmets, harnesses, ropes, and sticky rock-climbing shoes.

Also popular is a new and simpler version of this sport: bouldering. It's just scampering over rocks low enough to safely jump off. You'll find it's a fun team sport as you push and pull each other up and over the boulders. Regular hiking boots provide plenty of traction to grip the rocks.

DAY TWO: *Afternoon*

LUNCH

Hopping over rocks really builds an appetite. From your parking spot at the Barker Dam trailhead, follow the signs to the Hidden Valley picnic area. You'll find plenty of tree-shaded picnic tables. It's a cool spot to enjoy a midday repast, serenaded by the wind rustling through the Joshua trees.

After lunch, hike the mile-long loop through Hidden Valley. It was a favorite place with cattle rustlers in the 1870s, since they could easily hide their pilfered herds in this expansive valley ringed by forbidding, rocky hills. The valley offered plenty of vegetation for hungry cattle—and privacy. The rustlers rebranded the beasts and often sold them back to their original owners.

Spend the rest of the afternoon hiking among the rocks (taking care not to get lost). You can watch the sun sink behind the Little San Bernardino Mountains, burnishing the rocks and boulders of Joshua Tree shades of warm desert gold. As an added bonus, you may glimpse a lone coyote loping across the valley floor.

DAY TWO: *Evening*

Returning to the inn, you'll be ready for a dip in the pool. As you float in the water, look up and watch the stars come out.

DINNER

Plan a low-key dinner at **Arturo's Mexican Restaurant** (61695 Twentynine Palms Highway; 760–366–2719; inexpensive). Relax over enchiladas, tacos, *carne asada,* and a couple of beers in the casual, family-style restaurant. Even better, order your food to go and dine under the stars at the inn.

After dinner, take in Joshua Tree's version of the performance arts at the **Hi-Desert Playhouse** (61231 Twentynine Palms Highway; 760–366–3777; $10 per person), which offers revivals of Old West melodramas, comedies, and more current works. If, however, your high-desert adventure isn't complete with an evening at a honky-tonk, drive west on Twentynine Palms Highway to the community of Yucca Valley, then follow the signs to Pioneertown. It was built in the 1940s as a movie set for Gene Autry and Roy Rogers westerns (and more recently *The Life and Times of Judge Roy Bean,* starring Paul Newman). The draw here is **Pappy & Harriet's Palace** (53688 Pioneertown Road; 760–365–5956). Open Thursday through Sunday, this saloon serves up Tex-Mex grub, line dancing, and live music. Not a bad spot to grab your sweetheart and take a spin two-steppin'.

DAY THREE: *Morning*

BREAKFAST

Have breakfast at the inn, and then take advantage of the cool morning for a hike to **49 Palms Oasis.** Park at the end of Canyon Road (off Twentynine Palms Highway, 4 miles west of Twentynine Palms) and follow this moderately challenging trail to an oasis of fan palms and pools (if there's been enough rain). It's 3 miles round-trip and takes two to three hours, depending how fast you trek.

After your morning hike, hit the road for home—with a couple of fun detours along the way. Stop at tacky-cool **Cactus Mart** (49889 Twentynine

Palms Highway; 760-363-6076) in Morongo Valley to pick up a souvenir of your trip—maybe a baby Joshua tree for $15. **Big Morongo Canyon Preserve Reserve** (follow the signs off Highway 62 on your way out of town; 760-363-7190) is another pleasant detour. A year-round stream makes it a natural oasis in the desert that attracts birds, frogs, coyotes, foxes, and other wildlife.

DAY THREE: *Afternoon*

 As you drive south on Twentynine Palms Highway, take the Desert Hot Springs exit east to the sleepy town of inexpensive hot springs "resorts." The **Desert Hot Springs Spa Hotel** (10805 Palm Drive; 760-329-7000 or 800-808-7727) is an ideal spot for lunch and an afternoon of well-deserved pampering. Daily spa rates are just $3.00 to $7.00, depending on the day, for unlimited use of eight mineral pools. Have a light lunch in the spa restaurant (inexpensive), and then claim a couple of lounge chairs under the shade of a palm tree. If soaking in hot, pristine mineral water (pumped from 3,000 feet below ground) doesn't soothe muscles sore from hiking, a spa treatment will. Services range from massages to mud wraps to facials; fees start at $30.

You could lounge at the spa until 10:00 P.M. (a pleasant thought on warm nights). Eventually you'll have to rouse yourselves for the drive home. No matter, the spa-induced bliss will carry you though the trip.

FOR MORE ROMANCE

For a contrasting desert experience, combine this itinerary with a couple of nights in Palm Springs, long a favorite movie-star playground. Book a room at the seventy-four-room **Estrella Inn** (415 South Belardo Road; 760-320-4117 or 800-237-3687; $115-$350), a restored 1930s-era hideaway. Even more intimate is the eight-room **Willow Historic Palm Springs Inn** (412 West Tahquitz Canyon Way; 760-320-0771 or 800-966-9697; $175-$500), where rooms feature fireplaces, private gardens, and plenty of privacy. For more information about attractions in the area, contact the **Palm Springs Desert Resorts Convention and Visitors Bureau**, 800-967-3767.

ENSENADA, MEXICO

Make a Run for the Border

Border Town Escape
A Day in Tijuana

STEPPING OVER THE BORDER INTO TIJUANA, your senses are assaulted by the colors, sights and smells of the busiest border crossing in the world. Everything about Tijuana is different, and that is why it's one of the most popular day trips from San Diego. Tijuana's reputation precedes it—thanks largely to its days as a haven of easy virtue during Prohibition. In fact, the city supposedly takes its name from Tia Juana, a famous hostess who set up shop there. True or not, Tijuana exploded onto the international scene back in the 1920s with the opening of **Tijuana Racetrack**. Gambling on horse racing was prohibited in California at the time, so the TJ racetrack was an instant success. The Prohibition years only added to Tijuana's allure as a playground for grown-ups. That reputation still attracts millions of visitors every year.

These days TJ's glamour has tarnished somewhat, leaving a bustling city offering wonderfully cheap shopping, restaurants, nightclubs, and bars. It's still a party town, and even establishments like the Hard Rock Cafe have opened shop to cater to the party animals who flock south. This itinerary, however, focuses on the city's charms, with shopping, great food, and a fast-paced spectator sport that has its roots in Europe.

PRACTICAL NOTES: Getting to Tijuana is so easy. Just drive thirty minutes south of downtown San Diego on Interstate 5 and you'll run right into the border crossing. We recommend parking in one of the many lots in San Ysidro on the U.S. side, then walking over (trust us, it's much faster and simpler than driving). Another option: Take the **San Diego Trolley** from downtown San Diego to the border. It's about a forty-five-minute ride; fares run from $1.00 to $2.25, depending on where you get on. The main tourist drag of Tijuana is an easy walk from the border, although cabs will take you there for around $5.00 (negotiate the fare before you get in). A word to the wise: Avoid Tijuana during

spring break, when the city is awash with teenagers taking advantage of the relaxed drinking laws. Weekends can be pretty hectic, too.

On your way back into the United States, Border Patrol officers will ask you to tell them your birthplace and may demand proof of citizenship—a passport, birth certificate, military identification card, or voter registration card is fine. While Spanish is the language of Mexico, you'll find English is widely spoken in Tijuana. In addition, U.S. dollars are accepted, and there's really no need to exchange currency. You can easily combine this itinerary with a trip to Rosarito Beach (Itinerary 20) or Ensenada (Itinerary 21), or both.

DAY ONE: Morning

Tijuana is a late-night town, so there's little point getting there too early—most of the places will be closed. Have a leisurely breakfast Stateside before heading south of the border.

Your nostrils will flare as soon as you get onto the Tijuana side of the border. Aromas from food carts mingle with car fumes to create TJ's unique fragrance. Visually, Tijuana is a jumble of buildings constructed with no uniformity or code and no apparent sense of layout. And therein lies Tijuana's charm. The city is an enormous contrast to her counterpart to the north. Whereas San Diego is orderly and planned, Tijuana is earthy and chaotic—at least to first-time visitors. Give yourself time to adjust your senses and tune in to Tijuana's wavelength.

Romance AT A GLANCE

✳ Shop at the stores along **Avenida Revolucion**, where you'll find everything from leather goods to textiles to pottery and silver jewelry. Don't be shy about haggling!

✳ Check out the open-air **Mexitlan** museum (Avenido Benito Juarez 8901; 011–52–66–384101). It showcases Mexican architecture in miniature Aztec pyramids, palaces, and villages.

✳ Have lunch at the birthplace of the Caesar salad—**Hotel Caesar** (Avenida Revolucion at Calle E. Zapata; 011–52–66– 851666). Or head to hopping **Tia Juana Tilly's** (Avenida Revolucion 701A; 011–52–66–859015).

✳ Admire works by local artists at the **Tijuana Cultural Center** (Boulevard Paseo de los Heroes and Mina Street; 011–52–66– 841111) in the city's Zona Rio neighborhood.

✳ Catch a fast-paced jai alai game at the Moorish- style **Palacio Fronton** (Avenida Revolucion 1111; 011–52–66–852524). Jai alai originated in Spain's Basque region and involves players catching and flinging a ball with wicker basket mitts.

✳ Wrap up your trip with a late and leisurely dinner at **Cafe Alcazar** (Via Oriente 9211; 011–52–66– 835030), located in the lobby of the Holiday Inn Pueblo Amigo. From there it's a short walk back to the border crossing.

The main attraction in Tijuana is the vast variety of stores, stalls, and *pasajes* (arcades) on Avenida Revolucion. And the shopping is duty-free, which means you can legally bring back up to $400 in goods from Tijuana without paying tax. With more than 1,000 stores to browse, you're bound to find a few irresistible goodies. And if you enjoy haggling, you've come to the right place. Most merchants don't expect you to pay the asking price and welcome a good-natured negotiation of give and take. But don't be rude—merchants are trying to make a living. Experienced shoppers aim to pay one-third of the asking price.

Many of the stores feature Mexican folk art of different types—be they traditional clothing, hats, pottery, artwork, lacquered boxes, jewelry, or ceramics—and of varying quality. Part of the fun is discovering what's good and what isn't. While you can bargain with many merchants, prices are firm at shops like **Tolan** (Avenida Revolucion 1111; 011-52-66-883637), which has a colorful selection of goods, but you can count on the quality. It's the same down the street at **Sanborn's** (Avenida Revolucion between Calles 8 and 9; 011-52-66-881462), which also has a wide variety of folk arts and traditional goods from all over Mexico. Down at **Mercado de Artesanias** (Avenida Revolucion between Calle 2 and Avenida Ocampo), you'll find an entire city block of stalls selling piñatas, blankets, sombreros, and pottery.

One of the delights of Tijuana's chaotic design is discovering its hidden gems. **Mexitlan** (Avenido Benito Juarez 8901; 011-52-66-384101) is one such place. This open-air, roof-top museum re-creates Mexico's architectural heritage. All sorts of buildings are depicted in 200 miniature exhibits—Aztec pyramids, temples, palaces, even whole villages.

For a glimpse at Tijuana's bygone glory, visit the **Ruinas de Agua Caliente** (Boulevard Agua Caliente y Tapachala 1202; 011-52-66-817811). The **Hipodromo de Agua Caliente** (Boulevard Agua Caliente y Tapachala 12027; 011-52-66-817811), the former Caliente Race Track, today is a venue for greyhound racing, not horses. The place has gone decidedly downmarket since the days when W.C. Fields, Norma Talmadge, and the Hollywood crowd came south to gamble. However, Caliente still has a thriving gambling crowd, and the two of you can try your luck on a couple of races.

DAY ONE: *Afternoon*

LUNCH

There's no shortage of great places to eat in Tijuana. You can dine on a bit of culinary history at **Hotel Caesar** (Avenida Revolucion at Calle E.

Zapata; 011–52–66–851666; moderate). It was there in 1925 that Chef Caesar Cardini created his eponymous Ceasar Salad—which is probably the best-known salad in North America. Another well-known TJ eatery is **La Especial** (Avenida Revolucion 718A; 011–52–66–856654; moderate), which features authentic Mexican country cuisine. **Tia Juana Tilly's** (Avenida Revolucion 701A; 011–52–66–859015; moderate) is another landmark restaurant that serves up seafood dishes, *carne asada* burritos, and other traditional Mexican favorites. Be sure to wash it down with terrific Dos XX beer (say *dose ek-keys*).

If you've had enough shopping for today, hop in a cab for a short ride to the **Tijuana Cultural Center** (Boulevard Paseo de los Heroes and Mina Street; 011–52–66–841111). The center looks like a giant beige golf ball rising out the Zona Rio area of Tijuana. It's actually a complex of galleries, theaters, an Omnimax movie theater, shopping arcades, cafes, restaurants, and bars—all under one roof. It's a great way to immerse yourselves in Mexican art and culture, be it photography, sculpture, or crafts.

DAY ONE: *Evening*

The fast and furious sport of jai alai is definitely a sight to see. You can't miss the Moorish spires of **Palacio Fronton** (Avenida Revolucion 1111; 011–52–66–852524) rising above Avenida Revolucion. Inside, jai alai is played on wood-floored courts with players catching and flinging a ball from wicker baskets with incredible force. It's a remarkably fast-paced game, and the Fronton still attracts top players from around the world. In its heyday, the likes of Marlon Brando frequented the Fronton to wager on the games. Matches kick off at 8:00 P.M. from Thursday to Saturday and last a few hours, making this exciting predinner fun.

DINNER

After the jai alai match, walk north on Avenida Revolucion back toward the border for a late dinner. Just before reaching the border crossing, you'll see Pueblo Amigo, a large complex of shops, nightclubs and restaurants. In the lobby of the Holiday Inn Pueblo Amigo is **Cafe Alcazar** (Via Oriente 9211; 011–52–66–835030; moderate). With fairy lights twinkling in the palm trees, this is a picturesque hideout for a romantic dinner. The menu combines traditional Mexican fare with Continental entrees—the light salmon is a favorite. Another terrific option in the Pueblo Amigo is **Restaurante Argentino de Tony** (Avenido Cenenario, Number 60;

011–52–66–828111; moderate). The clientele are mostly locals who come for the hearty, South American-style steak dinners. The restaurant's dark wood interior lends it a distinguished and upscale ambience, but the prices won't strain your wallet.

After dinner one or both of you may want to light up a Cuban cigar. You can buy them here and enjoy them in restaurants, but don't try to smuggle these contraband stogies back into the United States. There's a good chance they'll be confiscated, so if you buy 'em, puff 'em.

Of course, you can dance the night away till the wee hours at Tijuana's many discos. This border town boasts a thriving nightclub scene long after San Diego has gone to bed. The neon lights blaze along Avenida Revolucion. **Baby Rock** (Paseo de los Heroes at Avenida Rodriguez; 011–52–66–880440) is the wildest-looking club in town with a funky exterior that looks like a rock quarry. Inside there's a mainly young crowd dancing and pounding tequila shooters.

If that isn't your scene, however, it's a short stroll back over the border. When you see the line of cars waiting to drive into the United States, you'll be glad you walked. But, gentleman, there's one last purchase to make. Stop at a street vendor to buy a bouquet of cheerful, queen-size paper flowers for your sweetheart. They are a quintessential TJ item, and these blooms, like your affection, will never fade.

FOR MORE ROMANCE

If you visit between May and October, catch a bullfight at one of the two **Toreo de Tijuana** bullrings (one at Agua Caliente Boulevard and another at Plaza Monumental de Playas; call 011–52–66–801808 for information). This colorful, highly stylized ritual takes place Sunday afternoons at 4:30 P.M. It's a brutal show, but for some, the spectacle evokes the macho romance of Ernest Hemingway's *Death in the Afternoon.*

"Titanic" Romance
ROSARITO BEACH

IDWAY BETWEEN TIJUANA AND ENSENADA is the seaside town of Rosarito Beach. Named after the ranch that once flourished there, El Rosario, Rosarito is a weekend getaway favorite for Southern Californians. Just thirty minutes south of the border, it's as Mexican as you can get without straying too far from the States.

Like Tijuana, Rosarito came to prominence during Prohibition as a place where Americans could go for a drink without breaking the law. Central to that tourist trade was the Rosarito Beach Hotel. Today, Rosarito is beloved for its wonderful long, sandy beaches, great surfing, and delicious lobster. Inexpensive Rosarito provides a great-value escape with everything you need for a romantic weekend—fiery sunsets, terrific food, and a friendly, laid-back pace. In Rosarito, you can treat your sweetheart like royalty without blowing a king's ransom. Whether you choose to just kick back on Rosarito's terrific beaches or spend the weekend horseback riding, shopping, and golfing, you'll find this warm, friendly beach town a wonderful contrast to the bustling chaos of Tijuana.

PRACTICAL NOTES: Rosarito Beach can become ferociously crowded at the peak summer season, especially on weekends. Instead, plan your escape for a weekend some time from fall through spring. If you can get away midweek, local hotels offer some terrific off-season discounts. Driving to Rosarito is easy, but be sure to purchase Mexican auto insurance before crossing the border (American policies usually don't cover fender-benders south of the border). You'll see a number of drive-through insurance brokers in San Ysidro on the U.S. side of the border. Try **Instant Mexico Insurance Services** (223 Via de San Ysidro; 800–345–4701) or **Mex-Insur Inc.** (I–5 at the Via de San Ysidro Exit; 619–428–1121). Rates vary, depending on the length of your

Romance
AT A GLANCE

✶ Stay at the dress-down **La Fonda** (Highway I–D, Kilometer 59, La Mision exit; no phone) or the full-service, 275-room **Rosarito Beach Hotel** (Benito Juarez Boulevard in the heart of Rosarito; 011–52–661–20144 or 800–343–8582).

✶ Browse through the craft and furniture stores along **Boulevard Benito Juarez.** If you find something too big to fit in the car, merchants will arrange shipping.

✶ Have lunch with a spectacular ocean view at La Fonda's casual restaurant. Sip margaritas at the bar while you wait for a table on the terrace.

✶ Spend an afternoon lounging or horseback riding on the beach.

✶ Make reservations for dinner at **Chabert's Gourmet Dining Restaurant and Steakhouse,** a Continental-cuisine restaurant in the Rosarito Beach Hotel.

✶ Try a spa treatment at Rosarito Beach Hotel's **Casa Playa Spa.** The his-and-hers spa packages include massage, herbal wrap, and facial. Call the hotel for reservations.

stay and value of your car, but full coverage for a two-day stay runs about $30. Once you're south of the border, remember that you are in a foreign country and drive with care. Tales of police shakedowns of tourists for bogus driving offenses are largely overblown. Follow road signs and observe speed limits, and you'll be fine. Also make sure you have cash (U.S. currency is accepted for tolls, as well as at stores, restaurants and hotels throughout northern Baja) for the toll roads. These highways are the easiest and quickest routes into and out of Rosarito and are virtually empty—definitely worth the $3.00. They're also more scenic. Of course, since this is a beach getaway, be sure to pack swimsuits, sunscreen, towels, beach chairs, and anything else you want for a fun day on the sand. Finally, you can easily tack on an extra night and combine this trip with Itinerary 21 to Ensenada.

DAY ONE: *Morning*

To take full advantage of the day's sunshine, plan an early getaway after breakfast. To reach Rosarito, drive south on Interstate 5 to the San Ysidro–Tijuana border crossing. Make sure that you stop to purchase Mexican auto insurance before driving south of the border (see Practical Notes). Once you cross the border, just follow the Scenic Highway signposts for Highway 1D. You'll pay a $3.00 toll and cruise south on a well-maintained, very scenic road. From the highway you can take any of the Rosarito exits, which will drop into the beach town.

Rosarito has great shopping along Boulevard Benito Juarez, with more than 500 mostly family-run stores to browse. Bargains available are the leather goods, silver jewelry, pottery, and ceramics, and as

you venture toward the southern edge of town, you'll find a number of roadside stores and workshops featuring handmade furniture and cement decorations, such as fountains. As in Tijuana, don't be afraid to bargain with vendors. If you find a must-have piece that doesn't fit in the car, they'll be happy to arrange shipping. You can even order items to be custom-made.

There are several places to stay in Rosarito, but the most romantic is south of town, almost halfway to Ensenada. Rustic and family run, **La Fonda** (Highway 1D, Kilometer 59 at La Mision exit; no phone; $50–$70; cash only) is redolent with bygone Baja charm and romance. If you want reservations, write to their U.S. address: Box 430268, San Ysidro, CA 92143. Most people just wing it and try their luck when they arrive. La Fonda is a destination in and of itself, with just eighteen rooms spread among bungalows perched on the cliffs over the Pacific. For the most part, decor is rustic Spanish-Colonial; some rooms have fireplaces—a nice touch if you visit in winter. Many couples come to La Fonda and never bother to leave all weekend. After all, the hotel has a terrific restaurant and a path that winds down to a broad, clean, and blissfully uncrowded beach that's ideal for hand-in-hand strolls.

If, however, you prefer to know there's room at the inn and you want to be in the middle of all the action, book accommodations at the 275-room **Rosarito Beach Hotel** (Benito Juarez Boulevard; 011–52–661–20144 or 800–343–8582; www.rosaritohtl.com; $79–$379). The hotel has been a local landmark since the 1930s, when it catered to a clientele of movie stars and high-rolling gamblers. You'll find more old-time glamour in the older rooms in the original building, but more creature comforts (such as air conditioning) in the newer tower. The hotel also has a full-service spa, so ask about spa packages when making reservations.

DAY ONE: *Afternoon*

LUNCH

Even if the two of you don't stay at **La Fonda,** plan to have lunch in its moderately priced restaurant. Seated out on the patio overlooking the beach, you can sample the endless fresh seafood menu as mariachis play. In lobster season (September–March), it's heresy not to indulge in the sweet meat of the Baja California spiny lobster. Served Puerto Nuevo-style, these tasty crustaceans are fried and served split in two.

Where Jack Met Rose

It took an epic love story set in the frigid waters of the North Atlantic to bring balmy Rosarito Beach into the spotlight. Just five minutes south of Rosarito, in the tiny town of Poptola, is the Fox Baja Film Studios (011–52–66–140110; www.foxbaja.com; open daily 10:00 A.M.–6:00 P.M.; $5.00 per person). The oceanfront studio was built in 1997 for the filming of James Cameron's epic movie Titanic. The studio doesn't look like a tourist spot, since high concrete walls hide most of what goes on inside. But this is where Leonardo DiCaprio, Kate Winslet, and a cast and crew of thousands spent a year filming the record-breaking movie. Fans of the film can visit a Titanic museum housed in one of the soundstages there. For $5.00 a person you can walk through a First Class passageway, gawk at the huge boilers, and see costumes and other props. This is no glitzy Universal Studios–style tour—you can spend as long as you want.

Augmented with rice, refried beans, and fresh tortillas, and washed down with Pacifico beer or a margarita, this feast is pure nirvana.

After lunch you can walk off that big meal with a stroll along the long, sandy beach that stretches in front of La Fonda. Just follow the stone steps and pathway that wind down the bluff to the sand. In fact, you may want to make an afternoon of it and tote your gear to spend a few hours on this delightfully clean and uncrowded beach. Set apart from the party of Rosarito, La Fonda's quiet beach is a more intimate spot.

DAY ONE: *Evening*

DINNER

By now you might find that you've had plenty of Mexican food. For an elegant dinner make reservations at **Chabert's Gourmet Dining Restaurant and Steakhouse** (Benito Juarez Boulevard; 011–52–661–20144 or 800–343–8582; moderate). Next to the Rosarito Beach Hotel, this Continental restaurant is located in the hotel's original building. The interior is more akin to an elegant dining room, with its long drapes and stone fireplace that date back to the hotel's 1930s opening. Although you are in easygoing Rosarito, the menu here takes dining seriously. Appetizers include smoked salmon stuffed mushrooms and a wonderful lobster bisque.

Seafood is the specialty, of course, with lobster medallions in a cream sauce, salmon d'Chabert in filo dough, as well as steak and poultry dishes. Try to save room for the crepes Suzette or crepes Julissa made with fresh berries.

Of course, you can party all night long at Rosarito's many bars, or you can return to your room and let the sound of the crashing waves lull you to sleep.

DAY TWO: *Morning*

BREAKFAST

Enjoy a walk on the beach before breakfast, and then have a leisurely bite of breakfast at the hotel restaurant. Don't overdo it, since you'll be having lunch in Puerto Nuevo, birthplace of Puerto Nuevo–style lobster. Share a plate of Huevos Norteños (scrambled eggs with ham, bacon, and beans) or Machaca Norteña (scrambled eggs with shredded beef, tomatoes, onion, and green peppers).

Rosarito, being a beach town, demands that you spend time relaxing on the beach, and you may want to while away the morning on the sand. If you've always dreamed of riding horseback through the surf, you can do it here. You can hire a pair of horses in front of the Rosarito Beach Hotel (cost: about $8.00–$10.00 an hour). These aren't thoroughbreds, but you'll enjoy a nice gallop in the sand.

However, pampering of a different sort is available in town. The Rosarito Beach Hotel has a full-service spa, the **Casa Playa Spa**, offering affordable treatments that include aromatherapy, Swedish and sports massage, herbal wraps, body polishes, spirulina heat treatments, and hydrotherapy baths. Half-hour treatments start at $30, but their packages offer a better value. "Specially for Her (or Him)" packages start at $90, including a massage, herbal body wrap, and facial. Call the hotel for reservations.

DAY TWO: *Afternoon*

LUNCH

Is it possible to overdose on Baja's deliciously sweet crustacean? Fans will answer with a resounding "No!" Wrap up your Rosarito weekend with a

pilgrimage to the home of the Puerto Nuevo–style lobster. Puerto Nuevo is a small fishing village ten minutes south of Rosarito Beach—or at least it used to be. Now there are more than thirty restaurants serving these delicious fried lobsters with rice, beans, and tortillas. Visit between September and March and you'll sample lobster pulled from local waters. We suggest you head to Puerto Nuevo and try your luck—most of the restaurants in town do not take reservations (few even have phones), and come with cash, since not all accept credit cards. **La Casa de Langosta,** along the main drag of town, has all things lobster, from burritos to omelettes. For the best ocean view, make for the **Lobster House**. Lobster feasts run anywhere from $10 to $17, depending on how fancy the surroundings are, but anywhere you choose, it's still a great bargain.

When coming back from Rosarito, plan your drive to avoid rush hour. The slow crossing through the U.S. border backs up and at peak times can take more than an hour. On a Sunday plan to make it to the border crossing by midafternoon in order to beat the worst of the weekend rush back north.

For More Romance

Want to play a round? Baja California has couple of terrific golf courses just south of the border. The **Real del Mar Golf Course** (800–803–6038) is 12 miles south of the border on the Tijuana-Ensenada toll road, adjacent to a Residence Inn by Marriott. Greens fees are an affordable $49–$65 per person, including cart. Driving south from Rosarito toward Ensenada, you'll pass the **Bajamar Golf Course** (011–52–615–50151), which offers twenty-seven oceanfront holes. Greens fees are $60–$70, including a cart. Given the spectacular scenery and bargain greens fees, either of these courses is a treat duffers won't want to miss.

A Fishing Village with Style

ENSENADA

ESTLED 75 MILES SOUTH OF THE SAN DIEGO–TIJUANA BORDER CROSSING is the bustling town of Ensenada. Although popular with cruise passengers and college students who come to shop, eat, and drink, Ensenada is a genuine, thriving fishing village where you can watch the catch of the day brought in by colorful boats. The picturesque bay was discovered in 1542. Later, in 1602, Sebastian Vizcaino was so enchanted with the place that he named it the "inlet of all saints" or in Spanish, *Ensenada de Todos los Santos.* And the name stuck.

What makes Ensenada so much fun to visit is its hearty appetite to please visitors with inexpensive, great food and margaritas. You can set your own pace here. Relax and take it easy or join in with the party atmosphere at the nightclubs. Proving that it has something for everyone, Ensenada also has very well-respected wineries where you can sample the local product.

PRACTICAL NOTES: Easily accessible by toll road, the Transpeninsular Highway (1D) is picked up just outside of Tijuana (follow the road signs reading Ensenada Cuota). (For tips on driving in Mexico, refer to the Practical Notes in Itinerary 20 to Rosarito Beach.) The well-maintained, uncrowded highway takes you down the coastline, passing Rosarito Beach and Puerto Nuevo as you head south. From the toll road you'll watch the magnificent Baja coastline unfold with Los Coronados Islands just off the mainland in the Pacific. Taking advantage of its fine weather, Ensenada has a busy schedule of special events. Every February the town explodes in a frenzy of color-

Romance
AT A GLANCE

✱ Enjoy the drive south on the well-maintained toll road. You'll have the Pacific at your right and the largely undeveloped desert landscape to your left.

✱ Stay at **Las Rosas Hotel & Resort** (Highway 3, 2 miles north of Ensenada; 011–52–617–44310), just north of Ensenada. This thirty-one-room hotel has a dramatic setting high atop a bluff overlooking the Pacific—a perfect spot to catch a Baja sunset.

✱ Shop for local crafts at the stalls and stores along Avenida Lopez Mateos and Avenida Ruiz in the heart of Ensenada.

✱ Have a casual lunch at **Hussong's** Cantina (Avenida Ruiz 113; 011–52–617–40720), a local landmark and home of the $2.00 margarita.

✱ Sample the vintages of Baja's Guadalupe Valley wine-making region, just east of Ensenada. Or just stay in town and tour the **Bodegas de Santo Tomas** (Avenida Miramar 666; 011–52–617–78333). The region's mild, Mediterranean climate produces more than 90 percent of Mexico's table wine.

✱ Enjoy a romantic dinner at the French-style **Casino Royal Restaurante** (Boulevard Las Dunas 118; 011–52–617–71480) or **La Embotellardora Vieja**, the gourmet restaurant at Bodegas de Santo Tomas (011–52–61–781660).

✱ Drive 19 miles south of Baja to see one of Baja's natural wonders, **La Bufadora**. Waves crashing on the rocks in this tiny cove create a 50-foot-high geyser.

ful costumes when the pre-Lent Carnaval takes place. A garish effigy of Mal Humor is burned, marking the commencement of the celebrations. Cinco de Mayo (May 5) has become a big holiday, although more so for the visiting tourists. If you like seafood, the September Seafood Fair (in mid-September) is a great time to sample the local catch. And lobster season runs from September to mid-March—excuse enough for many Southern Californians to head south of the border. Of course, you can easily combine this trip with an excursion to Rosarito Beach (Itinerary 20).

DAY ONE:
Morning

Plan to leave sometime after breakfast. Ensenada is approximately ninety minutes south of downtown San Diego, and it's a remarkably scenic route once you get south of Tijuana.

There's a wide variety of hotels to stay in in the Ensenada area, but many of them lack that intimate and romantic touch. An exception is **Las Rosas Hotel & Resort** (Highway 3, 2 miles north of Ensenada; 011–52–617–44310; $132–$181), which offers a modern and luxurious retreat just north of Ensenada. Set high atop a cliff overlooking the ocean, Las Rosas features a spectacular free-form pool that appears to run off the cliff into the sea. Las Rosas is pricey by Baja standards. It's a luxury bargain by others. All thirty-one rooms have ocean views and private balconies or terraces—

your sweetheart will be captivated by the vast Pacific view. If you want to stay longer, ask about the two-night golf, tennis, and spa packages, which also include daily continental breakfast for two.

With its tennis courts, golf course, fitness center, spa, and, of course, that inviting pool, Las Rosas is so inviting itself that you may never want to leave. But that would rob you of Ensenada's hospitable charms. Drive a few miles south to Ensenada and make for the central shopping area of **Avenida Lopez Mateos** and **Avenida Ruiz**. It's here that the local arts and crafts are sold in a crowded and friendly atmosphere.

DAY ONE: *Afternoon*

LUNCH

Ensenada is first and foremost a fishing town. You don't need to visit the main fish market to get a sense of that because fresh fish dominates the offerings at every restaurant and food stand. Ensenada is the home of inex-

Den of Sin

*In the center of town is the **Riviera del Pacifico Cultural and Civic Center** (Boulevard Lázaro Cárdenas and Avenida Riviera; 011–52–61–764310). This grand white Spanish-Colonial building surrounded by elegant gardens and fountains was originally built as the town's casino and hotel. Indeed, serving Southern Californians drinks during Prohibition, the casino was owned by the notorious gangster Al Capone and managed by legendary boxer Jack Dempsey.*

pensive and delicious fish tacos, and it is the place for the best prices on fresh lobster (in season from September through mid-March). One of the landmark bars that you must visit is **Hussong's Cantina** (Avenida Ruiz 113; 011–52–617–40720; inexpensive), which has been in business since 1892 when German businessman Johan Hussong opened the bar as a stagecoach stop. For many visitors today Hussong's *is* Ensenada. The run-down-looking storefront bar might not look like much, but it is a local institution—and famous for its chili cook-off in September and year-round $2.00 margaritas. On weekends it's standing room only. The menu is a mix of fresh seafood, Mexican fare, barbecued ribs, and flaming hot chicken wings. Order several items to share.

In addition to its commercial fishing industry, Ensenada is the center of Baja California's thriving wine region. You could drive east to the Guadalupe Valley and sample the vintages at winery tasting rooms open to the public. Or just walk to **Bodegas de Santo Tomas** (Avenida Miramar 666; 011–52–617–78333) in the heart of downtown Ensenada. Open

Watch the Whales

From December through March the California gray whales migrate past Ensenada. These spectacular mammals swim relatively close to the coast, which means you may spot them from the shore. There are a number of whale-watching boats that depart from Ensenada's pier for an afternoon's excursion. Gordo's Whale Watching (011–52–617–83515) takes visitors out on the ocean, but call ahead to get a feel for how many whales have been sighted. Boats take passengers into the ocean for an exhilarating close encounter with the whales. Vessels typically also stop at Todos Santos Island for a glimpse of the sea lion colonies.

since 1888 it is Baja's oldest winery. Daily tours last about an hour—with samples, of course.

DAY ONE: *Evening*

After an afternoon of shopping and wine tasting, slip back to Las Rosas for a little early evening R&R. Definitely plan to catch the Mexican sunset from your ocean-view balcony. There's something spectacular about the way the fiery orange sun lazily drops below the horizon. Maybe it's just knowing you're in Mexico, but the sky seems a more vivid red and the sun seems bigger.

DINNER

Several places in town have a decidedly Gallic flavor, and the trick may be settling on one for dinner. For a change of scenery and for an overtly romantic atmosphere make reservations at **Casino Royal Restaurante** (Boulevard Las Dunas 118; 011–52–617–71480; moderate to expensive). The pink-and-white draped decor attempts to re-create the elegance of Louis XIV-era Paris, but with an unfussy Baja twist. The extensive menu naturally has lobster. In this case the signature dish is lobster thermidor, and they do an attention-getting shrimp flambé with Pernod and dill sauce. Finish off your repast with their stellar crepes Suzette. Just as upscale and surprisingly affordable is **El Rey Sol** (Boulevard Lopez Mateos 1000; 011–52–617–81733; moderate to expensive), an elegant eatery opened by French expats over fifty years ago. **La Embotelladora Vieja** (Bodegas de Santo Tomas; 011–52–617–81660) serves gourmet fare to complement its extensive wine list of vintages from north and south of the border.

DAY TWO: *Morning*

BREAKFAST

Why rush? Sleep in and breakfast at the hotel's airy, ocean-view dining room (the sumptuous omelettes are a house specialty). Then spend the rest of the morning soaking up the languid charms of Las Rosas. Play a little tennis, just hang out by that spectacular pool, or maybe schedule treatments in their spa. Massages and European facials start at just $25.

You don't want to rush your romantic getaway, so before driving north to the border, head south to the Punta Banda Peninsula and **La Bufadora,** home of the Baja blowhole. At La Bufadora—"the buffalo snort"—the rocks form a tight cove that creates the 50-foot-high geyser. It's a natural phenomenon—one of only three blowholes in the world—and you'll want to hold each other tight as you look down. Punta Banda also has a nice beach for swimming and snorkeling, so you may want to take dip. There's also a small clutch of shops selling La Bufadora curios, as well as silver jewelry, glassware, and shells.

FOR MORE ROMANCE

Being a fishing harbor, Ensenada's main waterfront is crowded with commercial fishing boats and cruise liners. Ensenada, however, also has three main beaches for you to stroll arm-in-arm. **Playa San Miguel** is 5 miles north of Ensenada. Just a mile south of town is the white, sandy **Playa Hermosa,** which leads into the **Playa Estero.**

For an interesting bit of contrast to Ensenada's beachy allure, plan a detour to **Laguna Hanson,** a mountain lake surrounded by pine forests and weird rock formations. It's located within Parque Nacional Constitucion de 1857—about 20 miles off Highway 3 from Ojos Negros.

THE MISSION INN, RIVERSIDE

The Good Life

A Vine Romance
TASTE THE GRAPE IN TEMECULA

God made only water, but man made wine.   **—Victor Hugo**

TEMECULA'S SUNNY VALLEY is the closest thing Southern California has to Northern California's Napa Valley or even the Santa Ynez Valley of the central coast. It's also a bit of a surprise for first-time visitors. Once you drive past the sprawling tract-home developments of this bedroom community an hour north of San Diego, you quickly find yourself surrounded by acres of rolling hillsides carpeted with vineyards and citrus groves. Wineries here are small and intimate, and when the two of you visit a tasting room, you're likely to find the owners themselves pouring samples. Temecula Valley is just coming into its own as a wine-growing region—it's still very much the new kid on the block in enological circles. While this getaway highlights the region's vintages and great food, you'll see there's also another, more down-home side to Temecula. If you believe warm sun and fine wine are the ideal ingredients for a romantic retreat, you'll be seduced by Temecula's charms.

PRACTICAL NOTES: Temecula is an anytime destination, but we recommend a fall visit so you can watch the grape harvest and relish the robust fragrance of fruit heavy on the vine. A word of caution: If you are driving from winery to winery, remember that it's all about sampling and *tasting*, not guzzling. And, of course, you don't have to hit *every* tasting room. Most charge a small fee of $1.00 to $6.00, which usually can be applied toward a purchase. You can request a map of local vineyards from the **Temecula Valley Vintners Association** (909–699–3626 or 800–801–9463). The association also can give you information about special events, such as barrel tastings, winemaker's dinners, and harvest-season festivities. If you prefer not to do the driving while sampling wine, there are options. To really do it in style, **Esquire Limousine Service** (909–694–0979) has Wine Tour

Specials for $180 per couple. If you're more active types, **Gravity Activated Sports** (800-985-4427) has a Temecula Wine Country Bicycle Tour for $90 per person. Groups meet at the Temecula Creek Inn and pedal through the vineyards to the wineries. Then everyone hops into a van to be shuttled from one tasting room to another.

Since Temecula is in the shadow of Palomar Mountain, you may choose to combine this trip with Itinerary 28 to the top of the mountain and the Palomar Observatory.

DAY ONE:

Morning

Set off sometime after breakfast, driving north on Interstate 15. On the way, make a brief detour to **Deer Park Winery** in Escondido (29013 Champagne Boulevard; 760-749-1666). They cultivate just 15 acres of vineyards, and the two of you can sample their vintages in the tasting room. But what really sets Deer Park Winery apart is an automotive museum featuring the world's largest collection of vintage convertibles and Americana—old radios, neon signs, Barbie dolls, and the like. Wine tasting is free; museum admission is $6.00 per person. From Deer Park Winery, you'll continue north on I-15. This stretch of North San Diego County is dramatically hilly and rocky, and you'll

Romance
AT A GLANCE

✷ Stay at eighty-room **Temecula Creek Inn** (44501 Rainbow Canyon Road; 909- 694-1000 or 800-962-7335) or the more intimate, six-room **Loma Vista Bed & Breakfast** (33350 La Serena Way; 909-676-7047).

✷ Lunch amid the vineyards and toast yourselves with a glass of sparkling wine at **Thornton Winery's Cafe Champagne** (32575 Rancho California Road; 909-699-0099).

✷ Spend the afternoon following Temecula's wine trail. A dozen wineries are tucked amid the rolling vineyards along Rancho California Road. Most have tasting rooms open to the public.

✷ Relax over dinner at the **Bailey Wine Country Cafe** (27644 Ynez Road; 909-676-9567), where the extensive wine list spotlights strictly local vintages.

✷ Kick up your heels at the **Temecula Stampede** (28721 Front Street; 909-695-1760). Nightly dance lessons offer city slickers two-steppin' tips.

✷ Start your second day with an hour-long sunrise hot-air balloon ride over the vineyards and citrus groves with **Temecula Valley Balloons** (888-695-9693).

✷ Spend the morning browsing through antiques shops in Old Town Temecula. The town's Old West roots stretch back to 1858, and this 6-block historic district preserves some of that nostalgic charm.

✷ End your wine-country getaway with a picnic overlooking the vineyards and citrus groves at **Mount Palomar Winery** (33820 Rancho California Road; 909-676-5047). Pick up a bottle of wine and a selection of cheeses and meats at the winery.

spot clusters of avocado trees clinging precariously to the steep hillsides.

Arriving in Temecula, you can check into your hotel first. The eighty-room **Temecula Creek Inn** (44501 Rainbow Canyon Road; 909–694–1000 or 800–962–7335; $120–$195) has the intimacy of an inn along with some nice resort facilities, including a twenty-seven-hole golf course, tennis courts, and an inviting pool with spa. Spacious rooms have golf course views with sliding glass doors that open onto private patios or balconies. If you want to extend your stay, ask about the two-night golf and wine packages. Prices start at $105 per person per night, including some meals.

Loma Vista Bed & Breakfast (33350 La Serena Way; 909–676–7047; $100–$150) has six rooms located in the heart of Temecula's wine country. In fact, this Mediterranean-style villa sits atop a hill, surrounded by vineyards with terrific sunset views of the valley. Appropriately, rooms are named after wine varietals, such as the Sauvignon Blanc, a Southwestern-style retreat with a private balcony, or the spacious Zinfandel room with a view of the Palomar Observatory. Rates include evening wine and cheese as well as a full champagne breakfast in the morning.

DAY ONE: *Afternoon*

LUNCH

Once you've settled into your room, make for Temecula's wine country. Just go east on Rancho California Road, and the strip malls and housing developments soon give way to the vineyards. Start your wine country adventure on a high note with lunch at **Thornton Winery's Cafe Champagne** (32575 Rancho California Road; 909–699–0099; expensive). Thornton produces a number of vintages but is best known for its Culbertson sparkling wines. Ask for a table for two on the patio, where you can enjoy the cool breeze and vineyard views while quaffing a glass of *cuvee rouge* and lunching on a seasonally inspired menu—maybe pumpkin soup in the fall or delicate fresh fish year-round.

After lunch, you may want to join a tour of the winery. Thornton specializes in *methode chamagnoise*—the French technique for making sparkling wine, which makes it unique in the valley. Across the street, **Callaway Vineyard & Winery** (32720 Rancho California Road; 909–676–4001) is Temecula's largest wine producer, with more than 700 acres of vineyards. Free tours are available several times daily from the winery's visitor center; tastings are $4.00 per person, including a souvenir

wineglass. Progressing northeast on Rancho California Road, you can stop at any of a dozen wineries. One of the prettiest is **Maurice Carrie Winery** (34225 Rancho California Road; 909–676–1711), which looks like a Victorian farmhouse. Samples here are free. Just off Rancho California Road, **Temecula Crest Winery** (40620 Calle Contento; 909–676–8231) offers tastings of up to four vintages for $2.50 per person. Sitting atop a knoll, the winery commands expansive views of the valley below.

By late afternoon, you'll be ready to head back to the inn for a nap or possibly a soak in the Jacuzzi while you watch the sun sink into the Rainbow Gap.

The Rainbow Gap

Environmentally speaking, Temecula is tailor-made to produce wine grapes. The Temecula Valley occupies a microclimate that means it's shrouded in fog in the morning—a cool, coastal mist that passes through the Rainbow Gap in the mountains—which gives way to warm, sunny afternoons. It's an ideal condition for cultivating temperamental wine grapes. In fact, Temecula takes its name from the Luiseno Indian word for "where the sun shines through the mist."

DAY ONE: *Evening*

DINNER

You don't have to go far for dinner at the **Bailey Wine Country Cafe** (27644 Ynez Road; 909–676–9567; moderate). The restaurant's low lighting, simple yet elegant decor, friendly service, and first-rate menu signal the upscale direction of things to come in Temecula. Now that the valley is beginning to earn a name for its wines, folks are turning their attention to food. Share a couple of appetizers to start—maybe a plate of paper-thin carpaccio and a pot of cheese fondue made with the Bailey Winery's chardonnay and locally crafted cheese. Entrees are a mix of fresh fish, pork tenderloin, chicken dishes, filet mignon, and pasta. The salmon Wellington—fresh salmon, roasted peppers, and shiitake mushrooms wrapped in puff pastry and dressed in cucumber papaya relish and accompanied by wehani rice and fresh vegetables—gives you some idea of the creative fusion of flavors you'll find here. Another feature that distin-

guishes the cafe: the extensive wine list is made up of entirely local vintages. Do save room to share a piece of Carol Bailey's rich white chocolate cheesecake.

Temecula does have a few après-dinner options. Sample Temecula's Old West side at **Temecula Stampede** (28721 Front Street; 909–695–1760; $5.00 per person cover charge), an enormous country-western nightclub in Old Town Temecula. You can two-step to live music or test your skill on a mechanical bull (you saw *Urban Cowboy*, didn't you?). If that's not your speed, the Wine Cellar Lounge at the **Captain's Cabin** (28551 Rancho California Road; 909–676–9334) offers more intimate surroundings for a nightcap.

DAY TWO: *Morning*

If you can afford to splurge a bit, put in an early wake-up call so you can meet **Temecula Valley Balloons** (888–695–9693) in the parking lot of Thornton Winery at 6:30 A.M. for a sunrise hot-air balloon ride. Hour-long rides cost $130 per person. It's a giddy experience as you rise over the valley's colorful patchwork of vineyards and citrus groves. In the distance, you'll see Palomar Mountain and Lake Skinner. Don't forget to ask the pilot to snap your picture together.

BREAKFAST

You'll return from your ballooning excursion by midmorning, and you may want to catch a late breakfast at the inn. Loma Vista B&B serves a full champagne breakfast. Staying at Temecula Creek Inn? Relax over a late breakfast in the Temet Grill while you enjoy views of the golf course and San Jacinto Mountains.

You saw New Temecula yesterday, so today you'll explore **Old Town Temecula**. This 6-block-long shopping district has its roots in the Old West. Back in 1858, it was a stop on the Butterfield Overland Stagecoach route. In 1998, the historic district underwent a multimillion-dollar renovation to gussy up its Western attire—complete with wooden sidewalks perfect for a morning's stroll. Old Town Temecula is best known for its collection of antiques stores. Definitely check out **Nana's Antiques** (28677 Front Street; 909–699–2389), an expansive shop of vintage clothing, china, and jewelry. She may find an irresistible satin art deco wedding gown, while he may find it hard to pass up a sterling-silver Victorian cigar holder. Also pop into the **Old Town Antique Faire** (28601 Front Street; 909–694–8786). This

warehouse provides space for forty-five dealers. Some of the more unusual items include antique phones from the 1920s that are in working order, as well as a selection of vintage cameras. If one of you has a penchant for timepieces, visit **La Casa del Tempo** (28465 Front Street; 909–695–3211). This small shop sells antique railroad watches, pocket watches from the 1880s, and old Swiss car clocks.

DAY TWO: *Afternoon*

LUNCH

Wrap up your visit with lunch at **The Bank** (28645 Front Street; 909–676–6160; inexpensive). This Mexican eatery occupies the former First Bank of Temecula, a circa 1914 building. These days, it's painted a sunny yellow. Sit indoors under the high ceiling of the former bank or out on the patio.

Another, more romantic option is to dip back into the wine country. **Mount Palomar Winery** (33820 Rancho California Road; 909–676–5047) boasts the most scenic picnic site in the valley. Pop into the tasting room to sample the wine, and pick up picnic fixings in the gourmet deli. A bottle of vino and lunch in hand, follow a short path from the parking lot to a hilltop picnic area, where you can spread out your feast on picnic tables.

FOR MORE ROMANCE

Cast a line to angle for trout, bass, catfish and bluegills at **Lake Skinner Recreation Area** (37701 Warren Road, Winchester; 909–926–1541). It's located about 15 minutes from Temecula; drive east on Rancho California Road and follow the signs to the lake. Day-use fees are $2.00 per adult. You can rent poles for $10 each and a fishing boat for $19 on weekdays, $28 on weekends.

Lifestyles of the Rich and Famous

RANCHO SANTA FE

L OOKING AROUND AS THE TWO OF YOU DRIVE EAST on Lomas Santa Fe Drive toward Rancho Santa Fe, you know you're entering a special place. To the south are polo fields and horse stables—a sure sign that you're approaching equine country. To the north are immaculately manicured golf greens. And the hills that rise beyond camouflage the estates of the real-life rich and famous. Indeed, Rancho Santa Fe is a champagne-and-caviar playground, but it is also a model of discreet taste and wealth.

Don't expect to find any "maps of the stars' homes" in "the Ranch." It's not that sort of place. Instead, Rancho Santa Fe has a sleepy feel. In the heart of the town you'll find a couple of delightful blocks of shops and restaurants, and a disproportionate number of realtors' offices (photos of mansions for sale—asking price $1 million plus—make for entertaining window-shopping). This itinerary encourages you to savor the community's relaxed pace and relish its understated luxury. After a couple of days exploring its winding country lanes and low-key yet deluxe lifestyle, you'll see why the likes of Jewel and Janet Jackson call it home. But don't go celebrity hunting—Rancho Santa Fe is so low-key that you'll never find them, and residents are tight-lipped about who really lives behind those high hedges and gates.

PRACTICAL NOTES: Despite being a high-profile zip code, Rancho Santa Fe is not a tourist spot. The locals are happy to let neighboring Del Mar and La Jolla

Jolla attract the masses. For the most part, though, the Ranch extends a friendly welcome to visitors. Casual attire is fine during the day, though you should bring some dressy duds for a fancy dinner. While driving through the town, though, keep an eye out for horseback riders trotting around. They use the same roads as the main traffic. It's easy to combine this trip with Itinerary 3 to Del Mar, possibly incorporating elements of Itinerary 2 to La Jolla for an extended taste of Southern California Gold Coast living.

DAY ONE: Morning

Plan to arrive midmorning and check into your hotel (they'll hold your bags if the room isn't ready). Rancho Santa Fe may be small, but it offers two very romantic options. The **Inn at Rancho Santa Fe** (5951 Linea del Cielo; 858–756–1131 or 800–654–2928; $120–$585) is right in the heart of town. This unassuming cluster of red-roofed, white-adobe buildings and cottages is surrounded by manicured grounds, including a croquet green that sees some action from the locals. The eighty-seven-room inn has a casual, relaxed air that's very old Rancho Santa Fe. The decor is sort of 1940s American Colonial meets Spanish Colonial, and it all works to create an unpretentious, residential ambience. Request a room with a wood-burning fireplace (about half have them), and for plenty of privacy reserve a garden cottage with a patio. Especially charming is the Agave Cottage (Room 133), which is a sweet, free-standing cottage with a little fireplace, hardwood floors and a charming Dutch door.

Romance AT A GLANCE

* Stay at the **Inn at Rancho Santa Fe** (5951 Linea del Cielo; 858–756–1131 or 800–654–2928), an unpretentious hotel in the heart of Rancho Santa Fe's village. Newer, more luxurious, and considerably pricier is the **Rancho Valencia Resort** (5921 Valencia Circle; 858–756–1123 or 800–548–3664). It's a wonderful spot for an ultraspecial celebration.

* Spend a few hours meandering through the village shops. Don't miss the **Country Friends Shop** (on the corner of El Tordo and Avenida de Acacias; 858–756–1192) for a first-rate selection of secondhand china, silver, and furnishings.

* Enjoy a casual Mexican lunch on the patio at **Bolero** (6024 Paseo Delicias; 858–756–5157). Start with a bowl of the delicious guacamole and chips.

* In summer, pass the afternoon watching the sport of kings at the **San Diego Polo Club** (14555 El Camino Real; 858–481–9217).

* Celebrate your courtship with dinner at **Mille Fleurs** (6009 Paseo Delicias; 858–756–3085), where Chef Martin Woesle creates an ever-changing menu.

For more gold-plated pampering, book a room at the **Rancho Valencia Resort** (5921 Valencia Circle; 858–756–1123 or 800–935–7846; $410–$3,500). This Relais & Chateaux property is a favorite hideaway for couples from Bob and Dolores Hope to Danny DeVito and Rhea Perlman. Accommodations are in forty-three suites spread over twenty casitas. The 850-square-foot Del Mar suites are the smallest, but with hand-painted tiles, terra-cotta floors, a fireplace and a spacious private patio, these make a very cozy nest for a romantic escape. Days here begin with fresh-squeezed orange juice, a newspaper and a rosebud left outside your door. One-night Romantic Getaway packages begin at $650, including champagne on arrival, a candlelight dinner served in your suite, breakfast served en suite, and a one-hour, in-room Swedish massage for each of you.

After settling in at your hotel, check out Rancho Santa Fe's small commercial center, where you'll find plenty of small shops, antiques stores, restaurants, and coffeehouses to explore. You could easily lose the morning in the **Country Friends Shop** (corner of El Tordo and Avenida de Acacias; 858–756–1192), which is Rancho Santa Fe's well-heeled version of a thrift shop. Complete sets of "previously owned" china, silverware, furniture and objets d'art are among the treasures you'll find here, and you can feel good about your purchase since proceeds benefit local charities. Need to pick up a little bauble to show your affection? **Beran's Estate & Fine Jewelry** (6016 La Granada; 858–756–4508) and **Marilyn Mulloy Estate Jewelers** (6024 Paseo Delicias; 858–756–4010) both specialize in top-quality used precious jewels and watches.

DAY ONE: *Afternoon*

LUNCH

After all that browsing and buying, you've surely worked up an appetite for lunch. **Bolero** (6024 Paseo Delicias; 858–756–5157; moderate) will put you in good spirits. This restaurant offers great margaritas and a nice variety of salads, fish tacos, tostadas, quesadillas, and other Mexican fare. On a typically warm and sunny afternoon, you'll want to take refuge under one of the umbrellas on the patio.

After lunch, hop in the car and discover some of the local places of interest. It might look like a modest vegetable stand, but **Chino's Farms** (6123 Calzeda del Bosque; 858–756–3184) is where famed chefs Wolfgang Puck and Alice Waters, among others throughout California, buy their pro-

From Railroad Land
to a Ranch for the Wealthy

Rancho Santa Fe is notable for its acres of white-barked eucalyptus trees. The area was originally purchased by the Santa Fe Railroad, which proceeded to plant 3 million trees as a source for the railroads ties. But the eucalyptus wood proved too soft for that purpose, and the railroad was left with a 4,000-acre forest on its hands. So, in the 1920s, architect Lilian Ross was hired to design an exclusive residential enclave to be named Rancho Santa Fe. What keeps Rancho Santa Fe so unspoiled and charming is the Protective Covenant of 1928, a series of building codes that govern residential and commercial development. The covenant has served the town well by preserving Ross's vision of a sleepy Spanish village. There are no McDonald's outlets here.

As the town was being developed in the 1920s, two Hollywood stars, Mary Pickford and Douglas Fairbanks, arrived and built a love nest. They christened it Rancho Zorro, after Fairbanks's smash film. Today, Rancho Santa Fe's newer annex, Fairbanks Ranch, is named for the screen idol.

duce. Dedicated foodies will relish a pilgrimage to this shrine of fresh produce. The fruits of the Chino family's Rancho Santa Fe fields have been chronicled everywhere from the *New Yorker* to *Vogue*.

Just a five-minute drive from Chino's is the **Helen Woodward Animal Center** (6461 El Apajo Road; 858–756–5545). Animal lovers will enjoy visiting the canine, feline, and equine residents at this no-kill shelter. If you find a new pal, be prepared to fill out an exhaustive questionnaire. The Helen Woodward Animal Center thoroughly checks the pedigree of prospective owners.

DAY ONE: *Evening*

DINNER

A balmy summer or fall night is perfect for a stroll into town for dinner at one of the San Diego area's leading restaurants. Tonight it's going to be something special (and for this occasion, price is no object)—**Mille Fleurs** (6009 Paseo Delicias; 858–756–3085; expensive). This French restaurant

has a delightfully warm and elegant decor. Inside, a brick fireplace flickers an orange glow on the proceedings, with the deep brown wood beams above completing the country inn feel. The menu highlights the talent of Chef Martin Woesle, whose dishes have made him the toast of the county. Selections change daily and feature produce courtesy of Chino's, of course. Fish, medallions of venison, roasted rack of Australian lamb, and stuffed quail are all part of Woesle's repertoire. A selection from an extensive wine list is the perfect companion for this repast.

After dinner share a nightcap at Mille Fleurs's lively piano bar or, for a quieter setting, retreat to the cozy bar at the Inn at Rancho Santa Fe. If it's warm, take a stroll outside—the Ranch's famous covenant means there are no streetlights, so you can enjoy some of the best stargazing in the city.

DAY TWO: *Morning*

BREAKFAST

Return to the town center for breakfast at **Thyme in the Ranch** (16905 Avenida de Acacias; 858–759–0747; inexpensive), where a tempting selection of baked goodies, omelettes, and specialty coffees awaits you in a small nook hidden in a courtyard off the main strip. If Thyme on the Ranch is too crowded, Mille Fleurs runs the **Cafe Mille Fleur Espresso Bar** in a quieter corner of the same complex. Order coffee and a scone to enjoy at a table beside the courtyard fountain.

Spend the rest of the morning luxuriating at your hotel. The Inn at Rancho Santa Fe offers three tennis courts, if you play, or you can just lounge together by the small pool. At Rancho Valencia Resort you'll find a first-rate, eighteen-court tennis facility. Sign up for a lesson with one of the eight staff pros and pick up some tips to play a winning game of doubles.

DAY TWO: *Afternoon*

LUNCH

Even if you didn't stay at Rancho Valencia Resort, plan to have lunch in its dining room, where Chef Steven Sumner's signature dishes include a sautéed ahi tuna roll wrapped in spinach. Sit outside or request a table in

the cheerful Sunrise Room. It's decked from floor to ceiling in hand-painted tiles in Provençal shades of blue, yellow, and green.

Finish your trip with a true taste of Ranch life with an afternoon at the **San Diego Polo Club** (14555 El Camino Real; 858–481–9217). Polo season runs from June through September, and the polo matches are open to the public. The chukkers begin at 1:30 P.M. and at 3:30 P.M. every Sunday. General admission is $5.00 (and BYOB), but for $25.00 you can hang out in the Players' Club. Pop the cork on a chilled bottle of white wine and settle back to watch the fast and furious action.

FOR MORE ROMANCE

Golfers will find some terrific private courses right in Rancho Santa Fe, and your innkeeper can make arrangements for you to play a round. Bing Crosby held his first tournament on the challenging greens of the **Rancho Santa Fe Golf Club** (5827 Via de la Cumbre; 858–756–3094; greens fees are $125–$135 per player). Novice and intermediate players should try the more forgiving links at **Morgan Run Resort & Club** (5690 Chancha de Golf; 858–756–3255; greens fees are $60–$70 per player).

☉N a Mission of Love
A WEEKEND IN RIVERSIDE

UST OVER THE COUNTY LINE, TWO HOURS NORTH of San Diego and southeast of Los Angeles, is Riverside. In many ways, it's a city that time forgot. Once surrounded by citrus groves, today it's a college town and home to the University of California. But Riverside also has one of California's great historic hotels, the Mission Inn, an eccentric and captivating excuse for a romantic road trip. Built between 1902 and 1932, the inn is a vibrant piece of Riverside history that occupies an entire city block. With a unique architectural blend of Spanish mission and Asian influences, ancient bells and a clock tower with a funky glockenspiel, the Mission Inn yields surprises at every turn and secret passageway. This itinerary gives the two of you plenty of time to soak up the inn's Old California glamour, with a lively docent-led tour to learn its many secrets.

PRACTICAL NOTES: The inn has one of the most inviting pools in Southern California, so be sure to pack swimsuits. Riverside gets very warm in the summer, and you'll definitely want to cool off in the pool. Another great time to visit is during the winter holidays, when the hotel twinkles with thousands of lights. Since you'll stop at the mud baths at Glen Ivy Hot Springs, it's also smart to bring some old swimwear—the mud can really do a number on a bathing suit. On the way to Riverside, it's easy to stop in the Temecula wine country (see Itinerary 22) to taste the local vintages.

DAY ONE: *Morning*

After breakfast, plan a late-morning exit. It's a two-hour drive north on Interstate 15 to the **Mission Inn** (3649 Mission Inn Avenue; 909–784–0300

oe 800–843–7755; $129–$650). Looking like a Spanish Colonial mission, the inn was the inspiration of Frank Miller, one of Riverside's founding fathers. The inn's original structure opened in 1902, and Miller spent the next thirty years lovingly enhancing it with priceless antiques purchased in the United States and Europe.

Miller has been dubbed Riverside's William Randolph Hearst, and it's an apt comparison. Like the newspaper baron's beloved Hearst Castle in San Simeon, the Mission Inn is a curious mélange of architectural styles. "A monastery, a mission, a fine hotel, a home, a boarding house, a museum, and an art gallery" is how humorist Will Rogers described it in 1934. That's just as true today. Among the oddities is an enormous wooden chair found in the lobby. It was custom-built for President William Taft, a gentleman of behemoth proportions, for his visit in 1904. Bet both of you can fit into it. When you walk through the lobby, take a close look at the long rug that depicts California's missions. Chinese weavers misspelled some of the names. Throughout, the hotel is a fantasy of Moorish arches, Gothic flying buttresses, glorious tile and wrought-iron decorative details, and Spanish-style red tile roofs.

Romance AT A GLANCE

* Spend the night at the **Mission Inn** (3649 Mission Inn Avenue; 909–784–0300 or 800–843–7755), a National Historic Landmark that's a symbol of Riverside. Ask about their special romance and celebration packages.

* After check-in, join a docent-led tour of the hotel, which is filled with more than $5 million in art and antiques and has hosted presidents and movie stars.

* Plan a sunset carriage tour of Riverside's historic district with the **Carriage House** (3491 Market Street; 909–781–0780). Rides include two must-have romantic ingredients—champagne and chocolates!

* Dine on first-rate steaks at **Duane's Prime Steaks** (909–341–6767), the hotel's signature restaurant. After dinner, have a nightcap in the intimate Presidential Lounge, where Richard and Pat Nixon exchanged their vows.

* Have breakfast, or a late brunch, by the fountain on the romantic Spanish Patio. Surrounded by brightly painted tiles, lush gardens, and the inn's collection of ancient bells, you'll think you're in Andalusia. Spend the rest of the morning lounging by the inn's palm-shaded El Agua Azul pool.

* On your way home, spend the afternoon at **Glen Ivy Hot Springs Spa** (25000 Glen Ivy Road; 800–454–8772). "Club Mud" is a Southern California institution, where you can bake in skin-pampering clay mud and soak in mineral pools.

You'll find some charming touches in your room, starting with a giant door that looks like it opens into a monastery cell. Don't worry, rooms are comfortably furnished, though the dark wood-beam ceilings will make you feel like you're staying in a converted mission. Among the most interesting of the hotel's 235 rooms are those along Author's Row. Named for the writers, poets, and lyricists who stayed there in the 1920s and 1930s (including Pulitzer Prize–winning novelist Zona Gale, who was Miller's biographer), these rooms overlook the Spanish Patio and Anton's Clock and Glockenspiel, which stages quite a show every hour).

DAY ONE: *Afternoon*

LUNCH

After checking into the hotel, you may be hungry for a spot of lunch. Across the street, **Simple Simon's** (3639 Main Street; 909–369–6030; inexpensive to moderate) is a local favorite, thanks to their fresh bread and pastries. Try the roast lamb sandwich with roasted eggplant and red bell peppers, or maybe marinated chicken breast on fresh kalamata olive bread.

The Mission Inn Foundation operates the on-site **Mission Inn Museum** and offers fascinating docent-led tours ($8.00 per person; 909–781–8241; reservations recommended). The hotel has so many nooks and crannies that you almost need a guide to lead the way—and point out the more than $5 million in antiques and artifacts, including an amazing collection of church bells. The seventy-five-minute tour, offered several times a day, will allow a peek at treasures you'd overlook otherwise. Especially spectacular is the St. Francis of Assisi Chapel, a private wedding chapel with a seventeenth-century, gold-leaf altar from Mexico and stained-glass windows designed by Louis Comfort Tiffany. Also delightfully odd is the Cloister Music Room, which features a cathedral organ and pews modeled after London's Westminster Abbey. But Miller had eclectic taste, to say the least. His hotel may look like an authentic California mission, but he was also an aficionado of Asian art and culture. So he added the Court of the Orient and the Ho-O-Kan Room to house his Asian collectibles.

DAY ONE: *Evening*

One of the most romantic ways to get to acquainted with Riverside is by taking a horse-drawn carriage ride around town. The **Carriage House** (3491

Market Street; 909–781–0780; $90) will collect you at the Mission Inn for a forty-minute ride up the hill to overlook the city lights. In addition to the charming ride, you'll get a bottle of champagne, two keepsake champagne flutes, and chocolate hearts to nibble—and toast your union. Make reservations in advance so they can put a personalized message on the bottle's label.

DINNER

The Mission Inn has a wonderfully ornate dining room that's the perfect setting for a romantic dinner. Dress up a bit for **Duane's Prime Steaks** (909–341–6767; expensive), the hotel's award-winning dining room. Hearty traditional steaks and chops are the specialty here, but you'll find plenty of chicken and seafood dishes, too. Served by candlelight, it's an old-style repast, complete with duck consommé starters and baked potato and creamed spinach side dishes. Even the desserts have a traditional flavor: pecan pie, cheesecake, and the house specialty—rum cake.

After dinner, retire to the **Presidential Lounge**—aptly named, given its executive history. It was originally built as the Presidential Suite for President Teddy Roosevelt's 1903 visit. Replete with dark wood beams and intricate wood carving, it's an intimate spot for a nightcap.

DAY TWO: *Morning*

BREAKFAST

The Mission Inn is famous for its fabulous Sunday morning brunch (moderate to expensive), served in the **Mission Inn Restaurant** (909–341–6767) and on the Spanish Patio. Reserve a table on the patio, in the shadow of Anton's Clock and Glockenspiel. Start with champagne and Bloody Marys, then cruise the seemingly endless buffet table laden with seafood, desserts, pastries, and other goodies. Don't miss the made-to-order omelettes.

The inn's El Agua Azul swimming pool is a fine place to hang out under the sun for the morning. But in the immediate vicinity you'll find pedestrian areas full of boutiques, galleries, and antiques stores. Romantic movie buffs should make a pilgrimage to the **Fox Theater** (3801 Mission Inn Avenue, at Market; 909–684–2831). Opened in 1929, the Spanish Colonial Revival-style theater earned a place in movie history when it screened the very first preview of David O. Selznick's *Gone With the Wind*

Movie Star Weddings
and Presidential Honeymoons

Redolent with Old World riches and New World eclecticism, it's no surprise that the Mission Inn is a hugely popular wedding venue. Nuptials take place in the St. Francis of Assisi Chapel, the small St. Cecilia Chapel, or an outdoor gazebo. On any weekend you'll see flocks of brides and attendants bustling through the halls. The inn has hosted some famous bridal couples, too. Bette Davis said "I do" at the inn—twice!—and Humphrey Bogart married his first wife there. Two future presidents started their married lives at the inn: Richard and Pat Nixon exchanged their vows in the Presidential Suite (now the Presidential Lounge) in 1940, and Ronald and Nancy Reagan honeymooned at the inn.

in 1939. These days, the theater is home to the **Riverside Film Festival** (September–October).

DAY TWO: *Afternoon*

Check out around noon, and then head south on Interstate 15 to San Diego. A terrific detour is an afternoon at **Glen Ivy Hot Springs Spa** (25000 Glen Ivy Road; 800–454–8772; admission $19.50–$25) in the town of Corona. This is a fun place to relax and pamper yourselves in soothing mud and warm mineral pools. "Club Mud," as it's known locally, first opened its doors in 1890. Check in at reception, change into your bathing suits (bring a pair of old ones since the mud can stain; the spa has lockers for rent) and make your way to the mud bath. Sprawl around in the pool of red clay mud, caking yourselves in this skin-loving goo, and stretch out on chaise longues to bake in the sun. When you've had enough, scrub the stuff off and relax in the warm mineral pools, which come in several temperatures. Glen Ivy is a delightful spot to pass the afternoon. It has plenty of well-shaded lounge chairs and inexpensive sandwiches and salads for lunch. Wonderful massage, facials, aromatherapy, and other spa treatments are available for an extra charge.

FOR MORE ROMANCE

Heading north on Interstate 15 toward Riverside, you'll pass **Perris Valley Skydiving** (2091 Goetz Road; 800–832–8818), where daredevils float

down from the sky. This is the world's largest skydiving facility, and if you feel adventurous, pop in for a tandem jump. Strapped to an expert instructor, you'll soar into the great wide open from 10,000 feet up for the thrill of a lifetime. Allow three hours for the visit, which includes some basic safety instruction. Price: $199 per person for the jump and $75 for a video or photos.

If it's winter and you want some time on the slopes, spend Day Two in Big Bear, about a ninety-minute drive northeast of Riverside. This retreat in the San Bernardino Mountains has downhill skiing at Bear Mountain and Snow Summit, as well as miles of trails for cross-country skiing and snowshoeing. Make it a day trip (Southern Californians often play hooky to spend a day in the snow), or stay overnight at one of many lodges. **Northwoods Resort** (40650 Village Drive; 909–866–3121 or 800–866–3121; $129–$259) is a rustic, Adirondack-style lodge with some very nice amenities—in-room fireplaces, a heated outdoor pool, and a sauna. For more information about Big Bear, contact the **Big Bear Area Chamber of Commerce and Tourist Bureau,** (909–866–5753).

The King's Highway
A Train Trip to San Juan Capistrano

Yes, Southern California is a car culture, and the concept of public transportation is a novelty to many residents. But that doesn't mean you need wheels to see everything. For this day trip, just hop on the train north to San Juan Capistrano. The train depot is smack in the center of this small, walkable, and charmingly historic district in Orange County. You'll find one of the best-preserved Spanish missions anywhere, the oldest neighborhood in the state, and a marvelous sense of what life was like when California was a sleepy colonial outpost in Spain's expansive New World empire. Today it's a popular stop for tourists and locals, especially in March for the Festival de las Golondrinas, which celebrates the famous annual return of the swallows from their winter home in Argentina.

PRACTICAL NOTES: Trains ply the coast between San Diego and San Juan Capistrano from early in the morning until late in the evening. Call Amtrak at (800) 872-7245, to check current fares and departures. Fares from San Diego's downtown Santa Fe Depot are $22 round-trip, $18 from Solana Beach. The trip takes about ninety minutes from downtown San Diego, and just over an hour from Solana Beach. To spend more time in Orange County, combine this trip with Itinerary 6 to Dana Point.

DAY ONE: *Morning*

Catch the train from the **Santa Fe Depot** (1050 Kettner Boulevard; 858-239-9021) in downtown San Diego. Arrive a bit early to grab coffee

and pastries and to check out this Spanish-Colonial gem, built in 1915 for the 1915–1916 Panama-California Exposition. With a glazed-tile dome and gleaming polished wood accents, it's a popular spot for special events and weddings. Departing from North County? Pick up the train at the **Solana Beach Train Station** (105 Cedros Avenue; 858–259–2697). Designed by local architect Rob Wellington Quigley, the station's whimsical, postmodern style (it looks like an overgrown green Quonset hut, an interesting homage to the area's military history) has garnered international accolades.

Settle in to enjoy the journey through San Diego's coastal communities as the train chugs along the water and through Camp Pendleton, a Marine base that's off-limits to visitors. It's a relaxing commute, and you'll feel pretty smug if the traffic is bad on Interstate 5, which parallels the train tracks much of the way. If you missed breakfast, the train will likely have limited food and beverage service for a light morning snack.

Disembark at the depot at the foot of Verdugo Street in San Juan Capistrano. Stop at the information booth to pick up a map for a self-guided walking tour. The central village area is chockablock with historic buildings, and it's nice to know what you're looking at.

Follow the signs to the **Mission San Juan Capistrano** (Ortega Highway at Camino Capistrano; 949–248–2048). Admission is $5.00 per person (proceeds help fund ongoing preservation efforts). Plan to spend most of the morning exploring this historic gem. Founded in 1776 by Father Junipero Serra, the San Juan Capistrano mission isn't California's oldest (that's in San Diego), but it is the best-preserved example. Touring the mission's expansive grounds, you'll see that this was a thriving, hardworking community in addition to being a place of worship for the newly converted native people. After all, that was how Spain colonized California. Between 1769 and 1820, Franciscan padres established a string of twenty-one missions from San Diego to San

Romance
AT A GLANCE

✴ Take the train to San Juan Capistrano from downtown San Diego or Solana Beach.

✴ Travel back 200 years when you visit the **Mission San Juan Capistrano** (Ortega Highway at Camino Capistrano; 949–248–2048), built by Spanish missionaries in 1776.

✴ Have lunch under the trees at the **Ramos House Cafe** (31752 Los Rios Street; 949–443–1342) or the **Tea House on Los Rios** (31731 Los Rios Street; 949–443–3914), both in the heart of California's oldest neighborhood.

✴ Browse through the shops along **Antiques Row** on Camino Capistrano.

Rafael (north of San Francisco) along El Camino Real—the King's Highway. Each was overseen by just two padres and a handful of soldiers. The native people were converted to Christianity and made subjects of New Spain.

You can check out the Spartan barracks that housed a small garrison of soldiers in the late eighteenth century, as well as the simple quarters occupied by the padres. You'll also see where the Indians crafted soap, candles, leather products, and metal tools. The jewel of the mission is the small **Serra Chapel**. Built in 1776 it's the oldest building in California still in use and the only remaining mission church where Father Serra conducted services. The dazzling baroque altar came from Barcelona, Spain and is made of cherry wood overlaid with gold leaf. You can exit the chapel to the **Mission Cemetery**, where Juaneno Indians, Spaniards, and Mexicans rest in peace under the shade of olive trees. Nearby you'll spot the ruins of the **Great Stone Church**, which was a far grander house of worship than the Serra Chapel. Constructed by Indian laborers from 1797 to 1806, it was used for just six years until it was destroyed by an earthquake in 1812. Today the church is undergoing a ten-year, $20-million renovation.

When you exit the mission, you'll spot **Diedrich Coffee** (31760 Camino Capistrano; 949–488–2150; inexpensive), so take a break over an iced mocha. Camino Capistrano also is known as the city's Antiques Row, since it's home to more than a dozen antique shops. Take a look in the **Old Barn Antique Mall** (31792 Camino Capistrano; 949–493–9144) for a selection of American oak and pine furniture, china, pottery, jewelry, and crafts. Orange County is, of course, named for the citrus groves that used to dominate the landscape. Tin signs advertising long-gone fruit growers (about $25) are works of folk art that make terrific souvenirs.

DAY ONE: *Afternoon*

LUNCH

It may be on the late side, but that's OK. You'll miss the lunchtime rush at the **Ramos House Cafe** (31752 Los Rios Street; 949–443–1342; moderate), housed in a charmingly rustic, circa 1881 homestead. All seating is on a cool, tree-shaded patio—just the spot to sip a glass of homemade blackberry sage ice tea or lemonade. The menu changes daily and features a delicious selection of down-home items with a creative twist. Southern Fried Chicken Salad with Cranberries, Cornbread, and Pumpkin Seed

Goat Cheese Dressing is just one example. The desserts are a treat, too. Ice cream is made on the premises; Mark's Mom's Chocolate Cake is a sinfully rich devil's food cake adorned with chopped walnuts and bananas.

Across the street, the **Tea House on Los Rios** (31731 Los Rios Street; 949–443–3914; moderate to expensive) specializes in English-style tea. A pot of tea with finger sandwiches, scones, and other nibbles amount to a very filling repast. The menu also features salads and entrees, such as English pasties or curried chicken. Choose a table for two in the dainty dining room or sit out on the deck, serenaded by the fountain.

After lunch spend some time strolling through **Los Rios Historic District,** between Del Obispo and Mission streets. It's the oldest neighborhood in California, and three of the adobes date back to 1794. Adobes may be made of modest mud-and-straw bricks, but they are remarkably efficient—they stay toasty during winter and cool in the summer. You'll also see simple board-and-batten homes dating from the late nineteenth and early twentieth century. Most are private homes, so you'll have to admire them from the street. Perhaps the most remarkable is the **Rios Adobe** (31781 Los Rios Street), which was built by Spanish soldier Feliciano Rios in 1794. It's currently occupied

Forbidden Romance

The ruins of the Great Stone Church are home to the ghost of Magdalena. The daughter of a high-ranking Spanish official, she fell in love with the mission's gardener. It was a secret romance because of the difference in their social rank. But they were discovered, and Magdalena was commanded to do penance for her sin. Sadly, she was in the Great Stone Church on December 8, 1812, when it collapsed during the earthquake. Magdalena was killed, along with forty other parishioners. Mission staffers say they see the light of a burning candle floating through the ruins on the anniversary of her death every year.

by the eleventh generation of the Rios family, making this by far the oldest residence in the state continuously occupied by one family. Open to the public, the **O'Neill Museum** (31831 Los Rios Street; 949–493–8444) houses the San Juan Historical Society, as well as exhibits. Hours are Tuesday through Friday 9:00 A.M. to 12:00 P.M. and 1:00 to 4:00 P.M., Sunday 12:00 to 3:00 P.M.

DAY ONE: *Evening*

DINNER

You can catch the train back to San Diego whenever you're ready. Evening departures are at 5:53 P.M., 6:47 P.M., 6:56 P.M., 9:01 P.M., and 11:31 P.M. To soak up more old California history, plan to have dinner at **El Adobe de Capistrano** (31891 Camino Capistrano; 949–493–1163; moderate). This local landmark occupies a Spanish adobe that dates back to 1778 and was a favorite eatery of President Richard Nixon. He always made a point of eating there when he was in residence at the Western White House in near-by San Clemente. Expect traditional California–Mexican fare—tamales, chiles rellenos, and enchiladas smothered in cheese and a mildly hot sauce.

FOR MORE ROMANCE

Catch a free evening performance in the courtyard of the **San Juan Capistrano Regional Library** (31495 El Camino Real; 949–248–7469). Designed by renowned architect Michael Graves, the library embraces Graves's signature postmodern style while paying tribute to the neighboring mission. Musicians come from all over the world to perform at the library. Whatever is on the schedule is bound to be intriguing and worth taking a late train home.

FOUR SEASONS RESORT AVIARA, CARLSBAD

Fit for Love

$\mathcal{L}$ove $\mathcal{P}$edals

CYCLING DOWN THE COAST

ROM MARINE-TOWN OCEANSIDE TO SURF-SIDE ENCINITAS to chic La Jolla, San Diego County's beach communities all have their own personalities. To get a feel for all of them in one go, you'll want to rent a couple of bicycles and hit the road. Sandy beaches, dramatic cliffs, beautiful parks, and great cafes make for welcome stops along the way. On this itinerary you'll hug the coast while pedaling south. In fact, this trail is a "best of San Diego" wrapped up in a day's excursion. It's an affordable day, too, since you'll only need to shell out for bike rentals (if you don't have your own wheels), train fare from San Diego to Oceanside, and maybe a few refueling stops at cafes en route. The million-dollar ocean vistas are free.

PRACTICAL NOTES: This itinerary assumes you're staying at a hotel in downtown San Diego, perhaps the Horton Grand or the Westgate Hotel (see Itinerary 7) or the San Diego Marriott (see Itinerary 29). All three are a short pedal to the train station. To make this journey as easy as possible, take your bikes and catch an early morning train from the downtown Santa Fe Depot to Oceanside, some 35 miles north. That will give you all day to meander south at your own pace. One of you should bring a small back-pack to stash sunscreen and snacks. The beaches along the way are pretty tempting, so bring swimsuits and towels in case you want to take a dip. Most beaches have rest rooms or changing rooms so you won't be stuck pedaling in wet bathing suits. If you run out of steam along the way, don't worry, there are stops where you can catch the Coaster (San Diego's commuter train) back home. For some ideas on what to look for in the individual communities, check out the itineraries for Carlsbad (Itinerary 4),

Del Mar (Itinerary 3), La Jolla (Itinerary 2), and Mission Beach (Itinerary 5).

DAY ONE: Morning

First things first. If you don't have bikes, rent them in San Diego from **Bike Tours** (509 Fifth Avenue; 619–238–2444). They have a selection of road bikes, mountain bikes, and hybrids— any type will do for this journey. All-day rates, from 8:00 A.M. to 5:00 P.M., are $15, but opt for the 24-hour rate of $18 so you don't have to rush to return the bikes at the end of the day. Rental includes helmets, locks, road maps, and roadside assistance if you run into any trouble. They'll even deliver the bikes to your hotel at no charge.

Bikes in tow, at downtown **Santa Fe Depot** (1050 Kettner Boulevard at Broadway; 619–239–9021) catch Amtrak's San Diegan train north. The depot itself is a historic, Spanish Colonial–style structure dating to 1914. The cavernous waiting room evokes a bygone age when train travel was the only way to go. Service to Oceanside departs at 6:15 A.M., 7:10 A.M., and 8:45 A.M.; the one-way fare is about $9.50 per person. Call Amtrak at (800) 872–7245 for current schedules.

Ask the conductor where to stand to get on the train with your bikes (it's

Romance AT A GLANCE

✻ Don't have your own wheels? Rent bikes, helmets, and locks from **Bike Tours** (509 Fifth Avenue; 619–238–2444).

✻ Catch the train at the historic **Santa Fe Depot** in downtown San Diego for the forty-five-minute journey north to Oceanside. Call Amtrak (800–872–7245) for fares and times.

✻ Pedal south to the seaside village of Carlsbad for breakfast at **Hennessey's Tavern** (2777 Roosevelt Street; 760–729–6951), then continue down Highway 101.

✻ Cycle through the surf town of Encinitas. If you need a break, stop to check out the used-record shops and vintage clothing boutiques.

✻ Find nirvana, or at least pleasant gardens, at the **Self-Realization Fellowship and Ashram** (939 Second Street; 760–436–7220).

✻ Refuel with a healthy vegetarian lunch at **Ki's Restaurant & Juice Bar** (2591 Highway 101; 760–436–5236).

✻ Take a break and jump in the ocean at **Torrey Pines State Beach** (12000 North Torrey Pines Road; 619–955–2063), then tackle the big hill up through **Torrey Pines State Reserve**.

✻ Take a detour through the gold-plated community of La Jolla. Maybe pause at La Jolla Shores or the **San Diego Museum of Contemporary Art** (700 Prospect Street; 619–454–3541).

✻ Pedal along the rollicking boardwalk of Mission Beach, then follow the bike path on the banks of the San Diego River. Look for white egrets and majestic blue herons.

usually the far end of the platform). You can park the bikes in the vestibule, then relax to enjoy the journey.

When you arrive in Oceanside forty-five minutes later, fill up your water bottles, strap on your helmets, and start pedaling south on a gentle downhill grade along Coast Highway. Oceanside, as you'll quickly surmise from signs in merchants' windows, is a military town serving the marines from nearby Camp Pendleton. Cycle through town, and after 4 easy miles you'll reach Carlsbad. This quaint seaside town is where the Coast Highway really reaches the coastline proper and you'll get your first glimpses of the Pacific.

BREAKFAST

Carlsbad is an ideal spot for breakfast before continuing on. From Coast Highway, go 4 blocks east to Roosevelt Street and turn left to find **Hennessey's Tavern** (2777 Roosevelt Street; 760–729–6951; inexpensive). Among their omelettes and griddle specials you'll find their awesome Cap'n Crunch French Toast, which has enough sugar to power you all the way south of the border. If, however, you just need a great cup of coffee and a muffin to get going, then **Kafana** (3076 Carlsbad Boulevard; 760–720–0074; inexpensive) is the place to go.

In the Footsteps
of Triathletes

You won't be alone as you cycle beside the water. This path is one of the most popular routes with local cyclists and runners, including some of the world's top triathletes. North County is home to Mark Allen and Paula Newby-Fraser, two of the sport's best, and triathletes from around the world descend on the area for winter training. The balmy climate, of course, is the main draw, but there are plenty of challenging routes for running and cycling, as well as the Pacific for rough-water swimming.

Back on Coast Highway you'll ride south, overlooking Carlsbad's beaches, where local surfers take to the waves in all seasons. The next 4 miles offer a series of gently rolling hills that pass the Carlsbad campgrounds. The next community on the itinerary is Encinitas, a low-key beach town of surf shops, vintage clothing stores, and little cafes. If you like to shop for new and used CDs and records, stop at **Lou's Records** (434 North Highway 101; 760–753–1382). Just a few doors up is **Pannikin Coffee & Tea** (510 North

Highway 101; 760–436–0033; inexpensive). This two-story, cheery yellow cottage was formerly the old Encinitas Train Station. Now it's a favorite watering hole with residents and the flocks of cyclists who pass through. Stop for an iced tea, coffee, or baked goodie, or just browse in their gift shop full of decorative coffee and tea paraphernalia.

Three miles south of Encinitas's village, you'll come upon the golden domes of the **Self Realization Fellowship Temple and Ashram** (939 Second Street at Highway 101; 760–436–7220). This is where yogi Paramahansa Yogananda wrote *Autobiography of a Yogi*. This kind of thing may not be your cup of tea, but the temple's serene meditation gardens, complete with a small waterfall and koi pond overlooking the Pacific, are definitely worth a peek. Besides, it's free.

DAY ONE: *Afternoon*

LUNCH

After a long, straight stretch downhill, you'll enter Cardiff-by-the-Sea, a smaller community with a short stretch of restaurants on the water. Jump across the road to **Ki's Restaurant & Juice Bar** (2591 Highway 101; 760–436–5236; inexpensive), an invigorating spot with a great view of the Pacific crashing on Cardiff's pebbly beach. The menu is mostly vegetarian and quite good. Order a full lunch, or just recharge with a pair of refreshing juice smoothies.

Heading south again, you'll climb a small hill into the town of Solana Beach, which sits atop a cliff overlooking the ocean. If you're feeling weary at this point (approximately 15 miles from Oceanside), you can pull in at the Solana Beach Amtrak station and catch the train back into San Diego. This is your last-chance stop!

Ready to go the distance? Pedaling south on the Coast Highway, you'll come to the charming town of Del Mar. At the junction of Via de la Valle, it's a brief detour to cycle around the historic Del Mar Racetrack and Fairgrounds. Past the town of Del Mar is a long downhill stretch to **Torrey Pines State Beach**. This broad, sandy beach is a good place to stop and cool your heels in the Pacific. Ahead lies perhaps the day's greatest challenge—a long, steep, nasty hill winding to the top of **Torrey Pines State Reserve** (12000 North Torrey Pines Road; 619–755–2063). Drop down to low gear to pedal up, or walk your bikes up the hill and enjoy the scenic forest of rare Torrey pine trees.

Once you've made it through the reserve, you'll cycle past the Torrey Pines Municipal Golf Course, easily one of the most scenic public greens anywhere. Tiger Woods and other greats make a pilgrimage to these links overlooking the Pacific for the annual Buick Invitational every February. At this point, Coast Highway becomes North Torrey Pines Road. Stay on North Torrey Pines, turn right at the intersection and cycle past the University of California at San Diego. From the road, you can see the university's trademark mushroom-shaped Seuss Library building. Keep an eye out for the right turn at La Jolla Shores Drive, a welcome downhill coast (beware of the traffic) with stunning views of the Pacific. At Paseo Grande, hang another right and follow this road to the long boardwalk at La Jolla Shores Beach. If you didn't stop for a dip at Torrey Pines, here is another fine opportunity. At least buy a soda at one of the stands and pause to admire the view, which stretches from Scripps Pier (part of the world-renowned Scripps Institute of Oceanography) to La Jolla Cove.

From the Shores, follow Avenida de la Playa, and then turn right on Calle de la Plata as it winds around Paseo Dorado past the entrance of La Jolla Beach and Tennis Club (sorry, members only) and the Marine Room to Princess Street. There, you'll turn right back onto Torrey Pines Road. Take this one long block to Prospect Street, one of the main arteries through La Jolla. Keep an eye out for traffic as you pedal past shops and restaurants to the **San Diego Museum of Contemporary Art** (700 Prospect Street; 619–454–3541; admission $4.00). If you have time, pop in to see the museum's modern collection. Follow Prospect Street around to La Jolla Boulevard. This next 4-mile stretch will take you through the residential area of La Jolla's Birdrock community. If you're feeling adventurous, cut over a couple of blocks west to Camino de la Costa to see some of the priciest real estate in Southern California.

Once La Jolla Boulevard meets Mission Boulevard, you are in Pacific Beach. Traffic is heavy here, so take any side street 1 block west and ride your bike down Ocean Front Walk, Mission Beach's bicycle and pedestrian path. You'll pass Crystal Pier and continue south for 2 miles (keep an eye out for joggers and in-line skaters) to the Giant Dipper roller coaster at **Belmont Park** (3146 Mission Boulevard; 619–491–2988). Rides on this old-fashioned wooden coaster are $3.00 per person, and the view at the top is spectacular.

From the roller coaster head east on West Mission Bay Drive, but peel off on Quivera Road to avoid the traffic. Quivera Road takes you past a small marina and the Hyatt Hotel. As you continue south, it winds toward the San Diego River. Take the bike path that runs east—you'll avoid the car

traffic and see the white egrets and blue herons that call the river basin home. The bike path runs out and so you'll continue on Sea World Drive to the Fiesta Island junction. Make a right turn on Fiesta Island Road, which will take you over the freeway and drop you into Old Town State Historic Park. Take a brief break in Old Town, exploring the authentic Mexican adobe buildings.

From Old Town, your downtown base is within sight. The safest way back is to ride out of Old Town on San Diego Avenue to Noell Street, where a right turn takes you safely under the freeway to Hancock Street. Turn left and ride 2 miles south right back to where you started.

FOR MORE ROMANCE

After all that effort, why not surprise your sweetie with a little post-cycling pampering? Schedule a late-afternoon appointment at **Mirabella Mansori** (220 West J Street; 619–235–6865). One-hour massages start at $70 per person.

Tee for Two
A WEEKEND AT AVIARA

LUXURY AND SERENITY MAKE FOR THE ULTIMATE in romantic getaways. Tucked in the hills of Carlsbad, just thirty minutes north of San Diego, is the wonderful Four Seasons Resort Aviara. A golfer's paradise, this where the rich and famous come to play Aviara's challenging links. Tom Hanks, Steven Spielberg, and Bill Murray have hit on greens designed by golf legend Arnold Palmer, with views of Batiquitos Lagoon wildlife reserve and, in the distance, the Pacific Ocean.

But Avaria is much more than a golf destination. It's a place to indulge yourselves. Play a little golf, maybe rally a few balls on the tennis court, unwind with a spa treatment, lounge by the pool—recharge a relationship when you need a quick escape from the pressures of daily life. This is as good as it gets—if you can handle the price tag.

PRACTICAL NOTES: Four Seasons Resort Aviara is a platinum-card resort. Greens fees start at a steep $165 per person (including cart), but the resort offers a number of package deals that make an overnight getaway more affordable. Available midweek, the Golf & Spa Getaway package ($450 per night) comes with two rounds of golf; one round of golf and one one-hour spa treatment (ideal if one golfs and one doesn't); or two one-hour spa treatments. Celebrating a relationship milestone? Ask about the Special Occasion Package ($475 per night). It comes with chocolate-dipped strawberries on arrival, accommodations, a massage for each of you, and dinner for two in the resort's Vivace restaurant. It's a fine way to say "I love you." If golf and spa treatments are on your agenda, it's also a good idea to schedule tee times and spa appointments when making room

reservations. To see more of the surrounding area, combine this itinerary with Itinerary 4 to Carlsbad village.

DAY ONE: *Afternoon*

Arrive at **Four Seasons Resort Aviara** (7100 Four Seasons Point; 760–603–6800 or 800–332–3442; rooms $345–$440; suites $550–$1,750) by early afternoon to make the most of your time at the resort. Leave your car with the friendly valet and saunter into the gleaming, marble-floored lobby to check in. Be sure to request a late check-out tomorrow so you have plenty of time to hit the spa after a morning of golf.

Guest rooms at Aviara are made for romantic get-aways. Decorated in soothing pale shades of sand and ivory, they're spacious retreats with private balconies or patios, king-size beds, and palatial marble bathrooms. As a special touch, call ahead to the resort's **Isari Flower Studio** (760–929–0182) and order a lavish floral arrangement to be put in your room as a fragrant surprise for your beloved.

Romance

AT A GLANCE

✶ *Reserve a room with a view of the golf course or the ocean at* **Four Seasons Resort Aviara** *(7100 Four Seasons Point; 760–603–6800). To stretch your budget, ask about their packages.*

✶ *Order a lavish arrangement of flowers designed by the resort's* **Isari Flower Studio** *(760–959–0182) delivered to your room.*

✶ *Sink into a sofa in the lounge and indulge yourselves with a formal afternoon tea with scones, finger sandwiches, and petits fours. Or spend the afternoon sipping margaritas in the comfort of a poolside cabana.*

✶ *Have cocktails in the lounge, followed by dinner in the resort's* **Vivace** *restaurant (760–603–6999). Arrange for a bottle of chilled champagne to be delivered to your room for a late-night celebration.*

✶ *On your second day, after a room-service breakfast, head to the links for a morning tee time. Designed by golf legend Arnold Palmer, Aviara's eighteen-hole championship course offers plenty of challenges.*

✶ *Schedule postgolf spa treatments—maybe a sports massage or body wrap to replenish tired muscles.*

AFTERNOON TEA

The resort's refined afternoon tea (760–603–3773; 2:00 to 4:15 P.M. daily; $16.50; reservations recommended), served in the elegant Lobby

Lounge, is a wonderful repast. Order a pot of Lapsang souchong and peruse the tiered dessert trays laden with an assortment of finger sandwiches, petits fours, and scones garnished with thick Devonshire cream, lemon curd, and rose petal jelly. The lounge itself overlooks the golf course and has a wonderful fireplace and full bar. Sink into one of the sofas, or take your tea at a linen-draped table while being serenaded by a harpist. Simply divine.

The rest of the afternoon is yours to spend soaking up the Southern California sunshine. The resort's pool and two Jacuzzis overlook Batiquitos Lagoon and the Pacific Ocean in the distance. For the ultimate luxury, claim one of the white cabanas, which offer welcome shade from the sun's rays. Friendly pool attendants are there to handle any emergencies—fetch an extra towel, maybe, or bring margarita refills.

If you must insist on being active, Aviara's facilities include a tennis center with six courts. Or fit in a late-afternoon workout in the Fitness Center, where you'll find a full complement of weight machines, cardiovascular equipment, and aerobics classes.

DAY ONE: *Evening*

There's no reason to rush to dinner, so start the evening with a cocktail by the fireplace in the Lobby Lounge bar. Sipping predinner martinis while listening to live music is a delightful prelude to a romantic dinner.

DINNER

Vivace (760-603-6999; expensive) is Aviara's warmly elegant dining room with golf course and ocean views. On a warm evening, request a table on the terrace and dine by candlelight. Vivace's menu is Northern Italian infused with sunny California flavors. Specialties include mouthwatering risotto and seafood dishes (Maine lobster sautéed with saffron-infused sweet corn or Chilean sea bass served over bell peppers and potatoes with balsamic syrup and mint-scented olive oil are just two examples). Whatever you choose, save room for the *dolci*—dessert. These range from light, refreshing sorbets to downright sinful bittersweet chocolate melted over pistachio gelato.

While you linger over dinner, arrange for room service to leave a bottle of chilled champagne and strawberries in the room. It's a delightful way to cap off a languorous evening.

DAY TWO: *Morning*

BREAKFAST

Order breakfast from room service and lounge on the balcony in the morning sun (wearing the plush terry cloth robes found in the room's closet, of course) while savoring coffee and pastries.

If golf is your bag, Aviara is heaven. Arnold Palmer designed the environmentally sensitive, 7,007-yard, par-72 course, which makes the most of the natural terrain of rolling hills and valleys. You'll find expansive fairways, along with picturesque waterfalls and streams that double as confounding water hazards. In the distance is Batiquitos Lagoon, a natural sanctuary for more than 130 species of birds. It's scenery and challenges like this that make Aviara a consistently top-ranked resort course, and the Hollywood crowd frequently makes the pilgrimage south to play on these links. You never know who you might have to allow to play through on a hole. This course takes average players at least four and a half hours to complete eighteen holes. If you don't want to spend that long on the course, or you're new to the game, play only the forward tees, or just play the back nine. Either way, bet on the eighteenth hole to decide who picks up the tab for lunch.

DAY TWO: *Afternoon*

LUNCH

Coming off the eighteenth hole, you'll find that **The Argyle** (760–603–6908; expensive) is a convenient spot for lunch while rehashing your morning on the links. Upscale clubhouse fare makes up the menu. An ahi club sandwich on rosemary foccacia and the rock shrimp with white Cheddar quesadilla are among the more tempting items. Both are nice accompanied by a glass of the restaurant's California wines.

After lunch, cap off your weekend with spa treatments. Aviara's spa offers a menu of more than twenty to choose from, ranging from $55 for a 25-minute massage to $130 for an 80-minute facial, per person. A sports massage will work out any kinks you picked up from swinging a club on the green. If you want to know what a burrito feels like, try one of the spa's

body wraps. You're painted with a mineral-rich concoction of spirulina or mud, then wrapped up snugly in blankets to baste. Left in this embryonic state, you'll drift off to a blissful sleep. You'll both finish the weekend feeling mellow, relaxed, and revitalized. And isn't that what a getaway for two is all about?

For More Romance

Need help getting into the swing? Schedule a lesson for two with one of the resort's instructors ($40–$60 per person for a half-hour session). More serious players may want to join a half-day school at the **Kip Puterbaugh's Aviara Golf Academy** (760–438–4539 or 800–433–7648). These intensive, three-hour clinics are $150 per person.

Highway to the Stars
HIKING ON PALOMAR MOUNTAIN

"DON'T LET'S ASK FOR THE MOON WHEN WE HAVE THE STARS," Bette Davis implored in the film *Now Voyager*. Good advice. The winding road to the summit of San Diego's Palomar Mountain is indeed the "Highway to the Stars," earning this poetic moniker in the 1940s during the construction of the Palomar Observatory. It may be less than 60 miles from downtown, but it's another world. For one thing it's one of the wettest spots in Southern California with up to 50 inches of rain and snow a year. That means this mountain more than 6,000 feet above sea level is like a serene island in the sky. As you drive up the mountain, you'll break above the marine layer of clouds. It can be overcast in the valley below while the sun filters through a forest of pine and cedar trees at the top.

This day-long excursion harks back to an era when people took long Sunday afternoon drives in the country—not in a rush to get anywhere but just to savor the journey. You'll find this trip has a similar unhurried quality. Just enjoy the drive, spend a little time at the observatory, have some pie at a country cafe, and take a leisurely stroll on a mountain trail under the ponderosa pines. And like those old-time afternoon drives, this excursion is yours for the price of a tank of gas and a few inexpensive meals. The fine scenery is free. What better way to recharge your romance?

PRACTICAL NOTES: First things first. Palomar Mountain is truly the back of beyond in San Diego County, which means you'll spend most of your time on winding, two-lane country roads. Be sure the gas tank is full before you hit the S6 (you can fill up in Escondido). When to go? That depends on what type of experience you seek. The hiking is great from

Romance
AT A GLANCE

* Plan a morning departure for the scenic drive to the top of Palomar Mountain. Stop for breakfast at **Bakery Lafayette** (11828 Rancho Bernardo Road, Suite 105; 858–487–0418).

* Explore the **Palomar Observatory** (end of S6 road; 760–742–2119), with its massive, 200-inch Hale Telescope.

* Enjoy a casual lunch at a window booth at **Mother's Kitchen** (Junction of S6 and S7; 760–742–4233).

* Check out the treasures in the **Palomar Mountain General Store & Trading Company** (Junction of S6 and S7; 760–742–2496), which has an intriguing trove of jewelry, decorative objects and books.

* Hike across meadows and in the shadow of towering cedar, pine and spruce trees in **Palomar Mountain State Park** (760–742–3462).

* On your way home, feast on a down-home catfish dinner at **Lake Wohlford Cafe** (25484 Lake Wohlford Road; 760–749–2755).

spring through fall, but Palomar's high elevation means it's usually blanketed by a lovely mantle of snow throughout the winter. So bundle up, bring your snow toys, and spend an afternoon playing in the white stuff. Any time of year it's a smart idea to bring a couple of layers of clothing, since it can be chilly early in the morning and the late afternoon. If the two of you are amateur stargazers, bring a telescope along and plan to stay on the mountain after sunset. For more information contact the **Palomar Mountain State Park Headquarters** (Box 175, Palomar Mountain, CA 92060; 760–742–3462). You also can pull information off the **California State Parks** web site at ceres.ca.gov/dpr/. This one-day journey also makes a nice detour on the way to or from Temecula (Itinerary 22).

DAY ONE: *Morning*

You don't have to leave at the crack of dawn, but it takes about an hour and a half to get to the Palomar Observatory from downtown San Diego. For much of the way, it's a pretty drive on country back-roads, and you won't want to rush. Begin by driving north on Interstate 15.

BREAKFAST

If you skipped breakfast before leaving this morning, make a detour east on Rancho Bernardo Road to **Bakery Lafayette** (11828 Rancho Bernardo Road, Suite 105; 858–487–0418; inexpensive). Owner and master baker Jacques Auber fills his pastry case with tempting rolls, tarts, and French bread. Maybe order a couple of coffees and croissants for a lovely *petit déjeuner*.

After breakfast continue north on I–15 and take the Via Rancho Parkway exit east to Bear Valley Parkway. Head north on this road, which

turns into Valley Center Road (S6). You'll drive past the roadside antique shops and mom-and-pop stores of this rural community. Just follow the signs for S6, which passes through the warm valley's orange tree groves and eventually begins the steep, winding climb up Palomar Mountain. This is one of the prettiest routes in San Diego, though whoever is handling the driving duties will want to keep a close eye on the road. The passenger, however, will be delighted by the dense stands of oak, incense cedar, and Douglas fir trees that cover the hillside. Every so often there's a break in the trees through which you can see the mountainside drop toward the fog-shrouded valley below.

Follow the S6 road until it runs into the parking lot of the **Palomar Observatory** (760–742–2119; open 9:00 A.M. to 4:00 P.M. daily; admission free). Park the car and walk up the quarter-mile path to the white-domed observatory, which rises out of the meadow like something from of a 1950s sci-fi flick. In fact, it houses the 200-inch Hale Telescope, which can peer into galaxies a billion light-years away. Along the way you can stop off at the Greenway Museum to catch a forty-five-minute video about the telescope and take a gander at some celestial snapshots of discoveries made through it, such as the Orion nebula or the otherworldly Andromeda spiral. Astronomers have been gazing at the heavens through the Hale Telescope since 1948, and it's still one of the world's largest scientific instruments. You can climb the steps in the observatory to marvel at this giant feat of optic engineering, but, sorry, visitors aren't allowed to peek though it.

DAY ONE: *Afternoon*

LUNCH

Coming down the S6 from the observatory, you can't miss **Mother's Kitchen** (Junction of S6 and S7; 760–742–4233; inexpensive). It's the hub of activity in Palomar and the favorite food stop. The fare is strictly camping-casual—hearty chili, soups, sandwiches, burgers (you can even get a veggie burger if you want), nachos, and quesadillas. Order at the counter, then slide into a window booth. If it's a chilly day, you'll welcome a steaming mug of hot chocolate.

Next door to Mother's, the **Palomar Mountain General Store & Trading Company** (Junction of S6 and S7; 760–742–2496) is a bit of a surprise in this remote neck of the woods. Not only will you find groceries

and camping supplies, but owner Pascale Douet also has stocked his shop with an elegant selection of well-priced jewelry, small objets d'art, and books. Browse around and you'll likely find a trinket to surprise your sweetheart—maybe an elegant amber ring from the Baltic, a necklace of African beads, or a Roman glass paperweight. Or satisfy a sweet tooth with a few gourmet chocolates.

From the general store turn west on S7 and drive about a mile to the entrance of **Palomar Mountain State Park** (760-742-3462). This 1,683-acre open space has been a local treasure since the 1930s, when state park authorities created it to preserve "the most attractive part of the mountain." It's an uncrowded treasure where San Diegans come to play in the snow in winter and escape the heat in summer. It's also one of the most lushly bucolic spots in the county. If its neighbor, Anza-Borrego Desert State Park, glorifies the vast isolation of the desert, Palomar Mountain is a primeval setting of thick stands of trees and pretty meadows. Bambi would feel right at home gamboling in this Disneyesque setting. In fact, mule deer, squirrels, and raccoons do roam within the park. You can hike on trails shaded by sturdy, red-barked incense cedar, ponderosa pines, and big-cone spruce, as well as flowering dogwood, azalea, and wild lilac. Crossing the meadows in spring, you'll be delighted by the buttercups. Pick up a map at the park's visitor center and hike the easy 3-mile Doane Valley Nature Trail, connecting to the Lower Doane Trail and the French Valley Trail. This short, gentle route will take you along the Doane and French creeks.

DAY ONE: *Evening*

Stay on the mountain after the sun sets to do a little stargazing of your own. The clear mountain should allow you to see the stars scattered like sparkling diamonds across the sky. While Palomar Mountain is still a prime spot for stargazing, astronomers are concerned that pollution and light from Southern California's burgeoning development will ultimately impede this spectacular view.

DINNER

On your way home continue the day's backcountry theme with dinner at **Lake Wohlford Cafe** (25484 Lake Wohlford Road; 760-749-2755; inexpensive) in Escondido. Popular with local anglers, kayakers, and other water sports enthusiasts, the cafe is best known for its down-home catfish dinners—with unlimited refills.

FOR MORE ROMANCE

What goes up must come down, and a fun way to get down the Highway to the Stars is coasting on a bicycle. But who wants to pedal up? **Gravity Activated Sports Inc.** (800–985–4427) takes care of that little detail with its popular Palomar Plunge excursions. You'll meet the rest of the group at GAS's Pauma Valley headquarters, then ride in a van to the Palomar Observatory, where you get a tour of the Hale Observatory and Greenway Museum. From there you'll have lunch at Mother's Kitchen. Now you hop on the bikes for a 16-mile, 5,000-foot descent to the valley below. You'll hardly pedal the entire way. The price is $80 per person, including the tour, van transportation, bike, helmet, gloves, jacket, sunglasses, lunch, a T-shirt, and, of course, a photo.

If you don't feel like driving all the way back to San Diego, make reservations at **Los Willows Inn & Spa** (530 Stewart Canyon Road; 888–731–9400; www.loswillows.com; $195–$225). The luxurious, seven-room, forty-four-acre retreat is about 30 minutes' drive from the top of Palomar Mountain. You'll enjoy exploring the inn's grounds, which include a spring-fed lake, a private vineyard, an avocado grove, and plenty of spots for a romantic picnic.

Platinum Card Celebration

THE BEST OF THE BEST

AN DIEGO HAS SOME OF THE MOST BREATHTAKING SCENERY, finest restaurants and best hotels in California. With that kind of mix, it's been a playground of the rich since the nineteenth century when sugar magnate John Spreckels came south from San Francisco to build his dream house on the shores of Coronado. In the 1920s San Diego served as a Hollywood playground for the likes of Mary Pickford, Douglas Fairbanks, and Charlie Chaplin. It's still a favorite getaway for captains of industry (say, Bill Gates) and established movie stars. This two-night itinerary is divided between two terrific properties—think of it as a ritzy town-and-country getaway. It lets you live out a deluxe fantasy at some of the county's most exclusive haunts, where you can rub shoulders with the platinum card set. It's a touch of fantasy for most of us, but, yes, a few people really do live like this every day.

PRACTICAL NOTES: Work with the concierge staff at the San Diego Marriott and La Costa Resort and Spa to arrange special touches like in-room flowers and other goodies. If golf and tennis are on your agenda, don't forget to bring rackets and clubs (and to book court and tee times). For Day One's evening excursion to La Jolla, you may want to pop for a limo rental from **Presidential Limousine** (619–291–2820). Rates start at $209 for three hours, and it's a fun way to get around town for an evening. You can easily combine this itinerary with elements of Itinerary 2 to La Jolla, Itinerary 7 for Classic San Diego, and Itinerary 23 to Rancho Santa Fe.

DAY ONE: *Afternoon*

LUNCH

OK, so your personal holdings don't include a private Gulfstream jet. No matter. Pretend the two of you have just arrived in one at San Diego International Airport's Lindbergh Field. Make a nonchalant entrance—attitude is everything, baby—at the **Windsock Bar and Grill** (2904 Pacific Highway; 619-297-0866; inexpensive) and request a table for two on the deck. Hang out for lunch and a cocktail while you watch the airplanes come and go from the airport, with the bay glittering just beyond. And keep your eyes peeled—you never know who might be at the next table or passing through. Anyone who lands in a private plane passes through the Windsock. But no rubbernecking!

After lunch, head over to the **San Diego Marriott Hotel** (333 West Harbor Drive; 619-234-1500 or 800-228-9290; bay-view rooms from $195, suites from $475) down by the marina just minutes away. Check in and you'll be taken to your suite, which, twenty-five stories up, has the most spectacular views of San Diego. Thanks to the clear Santa Ana conditions, you can see all the way to the mountains of Mexico to the south and La Jolla to the north. Just across the bay you look down on the historic Hotel Del Coronado. The suites are huge and elegantly

Romance
AT A GLANCE

✴ Lunch at **Windsock Bar and Grill** (2904 Pacific Highway; 619–297–0866). It's located next to the private plane hangar at Lindbergh Field. Hang out on the deck, watch the planes come and go, and keep your eyes peeled. You never know who might land.

✴ Check into **San Diego Marriott Hotel** (333 West Harbor Drive; 619–234–1500 or 800–228–9290). Surprise your sweetheart with a bay-view suite overlooking the marina.

✴ For dinner motor up the freeway to the **Top o' the Cove** in La Jolla (1216 Prospect Street; 619–454–7779). Reserve a table on the heated patio overlooking La Jolla Cove.

✴ Enjoy after-dinner drinks in the **Whaling Bar** at La Valencia (1132 Prospect Street; 619–454–0771).

✴ Spend your second night at **La Costa Resort and Spa** (Costa Del Mar Road; 760–438–9111 or 800–854–5000). Ask about their one-night "Romantic Rendezvous" package when making reservations.

✴ Make the most of your day at La Costa—play a round of golf, enjoy a couple of sets of tennis, or just unwind in the spa.

appointed with to-die-for views (you actually have a choice of bay views or city views, but the bay side is the more romantic). Prior to arriving you'll have called to arrange for a spectacular flower arrangement to be delivered to your room (twenty-four hours notice is required for this romantic flourish).

Being based at the Marriott leaves you perfectly situated to take a gentle amble along the waterfront of the marina and into Seaport Village. Browse around the bookstore and coffee shop **Upstart Crow** (835 West Harbor Drive; 619–232–4855; inexpensive) and pick up a couple of bestsellers to read while sitting poolside later. Maybe sneak in a slim volume of love sonnets as a surprise?

If you want to be a little more active in the afternoon, the Marriott has tennis courts, bicycle rentals, and a couple of swimming pools (one being in a faux rookery with a waterfall). Alternatively, you can sit in the warm whirlpool and watch the sun drop slowly below the horizon while sipping a glass of chardonnay.

DAY ONE: *Evening*

DINNER

It's a fifteen-minute drive north to La Jolla from downtown San Diego, and the limo takes care of that if you chose to rent one for the evening. If not, drive along busy Prospect Street and pull into the valet parking at **Top o' the Cove** (1216 Prospect Street; 619–454–7779; expensive). This is an authentic La Jolla landmark, being set in a bungalow that dates back to 1884. There are three dining areas: the elegantly lavish dining room, the ocean-view heated deck, or the lushly planted brick patio that overlooks Prospect Street (the patio is popular with cigar smokers as it is one of the few places they can legally smoke these days). You'll want to reserve a view table overlooking La Jolla Cove. During the long summer days you can be there for dinner and still get to watch the spectacular blood red sunsets while enjoying cocktails. But location is only half the story at Top o' the Cove—the other half being the highly regarded menu. Appetizers include a choice of caviars (Beluga, Oscietre, Sevruga, or Imperial Malossol), or maybe you'll want to sample the sautéed scallops and saffron risotto with sweet red bell pepper vinaigrette. For an entree it doesn't get much better than the Côtes D'Agneau (oven roasted

lamb rack with roasted garlic, rosemary sauce, and herbed potato puree), although the Contrefilet De Boeuf Aux Champignons Sauvages (prime sirloin, pan seared with madeira, foie gras, and wild mushrooms) is excellent, too. And what's fine food without fine wine? Top o' the Cove has one of the most extensive wine lists in town (boasting more than 1,000 selections).

After dinner stroll down Prospect Street to the **Whaling Bar** in La Valencia Hotel (1132 Prospect Street; 619-454-0771). This landmark hotel has been here since 1926 and was once a stopping-off point for the Hollywood set on their way down to Mexico. Slide into a cozy booth in the recently refurbished Whaling Bar—a popular hangout with local movers and shakers—and enjoy an after-dinner drink, or drift into the lobby bar, sink into one of the plush sofas, and let the pianist serenade the two of you while you sip cognacs.

When you get back to your room at the Marriott, your view will have been transformed into a glittering array of lights. The San Diego–Coronado Bay Bridge is lit up below, as is the red roof of the Hotel Del Coronado. A cruise ship ablaze with twinkling lights may be docked in the bay. During summer months nightly firework displays light up the waterfront at the marina and SeaWorld just to the north.

DAY TWO: *Morning*

BREAKFAST

The view from the room is too good to miss. So have room service bring breakfast to your balcony. There's something sinfully delightful about that leisurely breakfast while you're still in your robe.

After checking out of the Marriott, head thirty minutes north on Interstate 5 to Carlsbad and the renowned **La Costa Resort and Spa** (Costa Del Mar Road; 760-438-9111 or 800-854-5000; $315–$470). They have a one-night Romantic Rendezvous package that features deluxe accommodations with champagne and strawberries to greet you, as well as unlimited use of spa facilities, for $350. There is top-flight golf on La Costa's two world-famous PGA courses, and there are the endless delights of the equally renowned spa. The two of you will be delighted by La Costa's fine cooking—which is especially prepared for health conscious-ness and taste—and the wonderful accommodations. La Costa is a real

getaway for the rich and famous, so you don't know who'll you'll bump into. The staff is very discreet, however, but you may spot Tiger Woods coming off the links or Bridget Fonda lounging by the pool.

DAY TWO: *Afternoon*

LUNCH

If you're busy playing racquetball or tennis, take a break for lunch at **Center Court** (moderate), the sports deli in the Racquet Club. For something a little more charming, however, visit **Brasserie La Costa** (moderate). This cafe has indoor and outdoor seating overlooking the golf course. The restaurant has both a regular menu and a spa menu that counts the calories for you without cheating on taste.

The rest of the afternoon should be spent under the expert hands of a professional masseuse as you enjoy a deep-tissue massage—or any one of the many spa treatments available to you. You can buy spa packages or enjoy them a la carte. Exotic herbal wraps, Roman pools, saunas, and Swiss showers are just some of the facilities available.

One of the benefits of the spa treatments is that you'll feel totally relaxed and exhausted. You can retire to your room for a well-earned afternoon nap, or lie out in the sun and perfect your tan. Or you can just float around in one of the swimming pools, keeping slightly cool in the afternoon sun.

DAY TWO: *Evening*

DINNER

Naturally La Costa features fine dining. **Pisces** (expensive) is the resort's fine-dining seafood restaurant. Of course, the fare is fresh and features everything from pan-seared swordfish in coriander sesame seed crust to live Maine lobster. Reservations are recommended.

If you're in the mood for Italian cuisine, book a table in **Ristorante Figaro** (expensive). The menu highlights grilled ahi carpaccio and linguine with sautéed bay shrimp, prosciutto, pesto, and pine nuts.

DAY THREE: *Morning*

BREAKFAST

Wrap up your luxurious weekend with a lazy breakfast in the privacy of your room. The extensive room service menu has traditional and spa-cuisine breakfasts.

FOR MORE ROMANCE

In car-conscious Southern California, you need the right wheels, right? You may not have your own plane, but you can rent a fancy jalopy to chauffeur your honey. A convertible Mercedes, say, or a zippy Ferrari will go a long way to complete this champagne fantasy weekend. **Exotic Auto Rental** (888–696–6842) rents those and more. Rates start at $155 a day for a humble Porsche to $275 a day for a Ferrari 308GTS. Call for reservations, and they'll deliver the car (at an additional charge, depending on availability).

Recommended Annual Events

JANUARY

San Diego Union-Tribune **New Year's Day Race.** San Diego Yacht Club, (619) 221–8400. Yachting enthusiasts welcome the New Year with a traditional regatta of monohull and multihull boats.

Martin Luther King Jr. Day Parade. Celebrated with a parade from the County Administration Building, along West Harbor Drive to Seaport Village; (619) 264-0542.

San Diego Marathon. Variable mid-January date; In-Motion, (619) 792–2900. Takes participants on a hilly, 26.2-mile tour of Carlsbad. Have Sunday breakfast and watch the thousands of runners pass by.

FEBRUARY

Buick Invitational Open Golf Championship. Second Monday in February; (619) 281–4653. Annual tournament draws the best professional players to the links at the famous Torrey Pines Golf Course.

Native American Days Celebration. Dates vary; Anza-Borrego Desert State Park Visitors Center; (760) 767–4205. Annual Cahuilla and Kumaya cultural celebration features demonstrations, lectures, nature walks and children's events.

Wildflowers Bloom in the Desert. Late–February through May, depending on winter weather conditions; (760) 767–4205. Wildflowers offer a colorful display in the Anza-Borrego Desert.

MARCH

Carlsbad Flower Field Spring Celebration. March; (760) 930–9123. Spring flowers create a rainbow of color on the hills of Carlsbad. Admission is $4.00 per person.

St. Patrick's Day Parade; (619) 268–9111. Colorful parade marches through Balboa Park and downtown.

San Diego Crew Classic. Last weekend in March; (619) 488–0700. Mission Bay is overtaken by international rowers who compete in this prestigious regatta; also bands and a naval parachute team.

APRIL

Gaslamp Quarter Easter Hat Parade. Date varies with the Easter holiday; (619) 233–5227. Spectators and participants don their Easter bonnets and watch a parade from Fifth Avenue to the Horton Grand Hotel.

Lakeside Western Days and Annual Lakeside Rodeo. Mid-April, (619) 561–1031. A cowboy rodeo, carnival, and parade.

Del Mar National Horse Show. April 23 through May 10; Del Mar Fairgrounds; (619) 792–4288. Olympic trials for dressage, horse and rider teams, plus national championship riders, draft horse, dressage, and western hunter-jumper competitions.

Sony Art Walk. Last weekend of April; downtown San Diego; (619) 615–1090. A walking tour of local artists' workshops.

Coronado Flower Show Weekend. Dates vary; Spreckels Park; (619) 427-8788. Largest flower show under a tent in the Western United States.

MAY

Tijuana Bullfighting Season. Sunday afternoons, May through September; Plaza Downtown Bullring and the Bullring by the Sea; (619) 232-5049. The traditional Mexican spectator sport.

Annual Fiesta Cinco De Mayo. May 5–6; Old Town; (619) 296–3161. Nonstop entertainment from south of the border.

Pacific Beach Block Party & Street Faire. Dates vary; Garnet Avenue, between Ingraham and Bayard Streets; (619) 641–5823. Live music, arts, crafts, children's activity area, a farmers' market, health fair, entertainment, and food booths—and it's all free.

JUNE

Annual Ramona Air Fair. Dates vary; Ramona Airport; (760) 788–6174. Features aerial fire fighting, aircraft demonstration flights, military aircraft flights, World War II aircraft, and aerobatic planes, plus vendors and food booths.

A Taste of Gaslamp. Dates vary; downtown San Diego; (619) 716–7146. Sample the diverse flavors in the Gaslamp Quarter's restaurants for just $20 per person.

Annual Deer Park Spring Concours D'Elegance. Dates vary; Deer Park Winery, Escondido; (760) 749–1666. Check out classic, antique, and sports cars.

The Del Mar Fair. Mid-June through July 4; Del Mar Fairgrounds; (619) 755–1161. Livestock shows, carnival rides, flower and garden shows, art exhibits, hobbies, and concerts by top-name entertainers.

JULY

The Annual World Championship Over-the-Line Tournament. Dates vary; Fiesta Island, Mission Bay; (619) 688–0817. Huge crowds gather to watch and play San Diego's rowdy version of softball.

Del Mar Racing. Late-July through early-September; Del Mar Racetrack; (619) 755–1141. First race is at 2 P.M. daily, except Tuesdays.

Hot Air Balloon Classic. July 4, Del Mar Fairgrounds; (619) 481–6800. Colorful hot-air balloons race in a graceful, airborne regatta.

Miramar Air Show. Last weekend in July; Miramar Marine Air Station; (619) 537–1000. Huge air show features the Blue Angels, with exhibits on the runway and acrobatics in the sky.

AUGUST

Fleet Week. Dates and locations vary; (619) 236–1212. Parade of ships, morning colors, fireworks, and a fly-over by the Navy Blue Angels.

Comic Con International San Diego. Late-August; Golden Hall; (619) 491–2475. Zap! Biff! Thwak! Holy comic book, Batman! It's the largest convention dedicated to all aspects of comic books and science fiction, complete with special guest stars, art shows and autograph signings.

SEPTEMBER

Street Scene. Dates vary; Gaslamp Quarter; (619) 557–8490. With four major stages and hundreds of music acts, this three-day event is the largest block party in the country.

Julian Fall Apple Harvest. Mid-September through October. Harvest, cider, and apple pie!

OCTOBER

Concours d'Elegance. October 15-19; Torrey Pines Golf Club; (619) 642–7469. One of the finest lineups of exotic and classic cars.

Oktoberfest. First weekend in October; La Mesa; (619) 440–6161. Bavarian-style festival of beer, bratwurst, pretzels, and oompah bands.

NOVEMBER

The Giant Poinsettia Star. Dates vary; Carlsbad Flower Fields; (760) 920–9123. A huge, red poinsettia star growing in the fields kick-starts the holiday spirit.

The Mother Goose Parade. Last weekend in November; El Cajon; (619) 442–6624.

DECEMBER

Christmas on the Prado. First weekend of December; Balboa Park; San Diego Museum of Art, (619) 232–7931. Free admission and holiday decorations, food vendors, and craft booths.

San Diego Harbor Parade of Lights. Held two consecutive Sundays in mid-December; San Diego Bay. Illuminated boat parade.

Special Indexes

ROMANTIC LODGINGS

EVENING DIVERSIONS

Cinema

Cocktail Lounges and Bars

Geographic Index

BALBOA PARK

Lodging
Balboa Park Inn (3402 Park Boulevard), 54, 56, 75, 78

Restaurants
Albert's Restaurant, San Diego Zoo (2920 Zoo Drive), 75, 76

Sculpture Garden Cafe & Bistro, San Diego Museum of Art (1450 El Prado), 54, 55

Attractions
Alcazar Garden (1439 El Prado), 7, 54, 55

Balboa Park Carousel (Park Boulevard and Zoo Place), 57

Balboa Park Information Center (1549 El Prado), 53, 58

Botanical Building (1550 El Prado), 54, 55

Cassius Carter Centre Stage (Village Place and Old Globe Way), 56

Japanese Friendship Garden (2215 Pan American Way), 55

Lowell Davies Festival Theater (1800 El Prado), 56

Mingei Museum of Art (1439 El Prado), 54

Museum of Photographic Arts (1649 El Prado), 55

Old Globe Theatre (1363 Old Globe Way), 54, 56

Palm Canyon, 54, 55

Reuben H. Fleet Space Theater and Science Center (1875 El Prado), 57

San Diego Museum of Art (1450 El Prado), 54

San Diego Museum of Man (1350 El Prado), 54

San Diego Natural History Museum (1788 El Prado), 57

San Diego Zoo (2920 Zoo Drive), 75

Spanish Village Art Center (1770 Village Place), 57

Spreckels Organ Pavilion (Pan American Road), 54, 55

Timken Museum (1500 El Prado), 54, 55

ANZA-BORREGO DESERT STATE PARK

Lodging
Borrego Valley Inn (405 Palm Canyon Drive), 7, 108

La Casa del Zorro Desert Resort (3845 Yaqui Pass Road), 108

Restaurants
Carlee's Place (660 Palm Canyon Drive), 109

Nightspots/Clubs
Fox Den (3845 Yaqui Pass Road), 111

Attractions
Anza-Borrego Desert State Park Visitor Center (200 Palm Canyon Drive), 107, 109

Borrego Palm Canyon Nature Trail (Hoberg Road), 108, 109

Grapevine Canyon (Off County Highway S-22), 112

Jasper Trail (Off County Highway S-3), 112

Warner Springs Sky Sailing (31930
California Highway), 94

RANCHO SANTA FE

Lodging

Inn at Rancho Santa Fe (5951
Linea del Cielo), 149
Rancho Valencia Resort (5921
Valencia Circle), 6, 149

Restaurants

Bolero (6024 Paceo Delicias),
147, 148
Mille Fleurs (6009 Paseo
Delicias), 5, 147, 149
Thyme in the Ranch (16905
Avenida de Acacias), 150

Attractions

Helen Woodward Animal Center
(6461 El Alajo Road), 149
Morgan Run Resort & Club
(5690 Cancha de Golf), 151
Rancho Santa Fe Golf Club, 151
San Diego Polo Club (14555 El
Camino Real), 147, 151

RIVERSIDE

Lodging

Mission Inn (3649 Mission Inn
Avenue), 153, 155, 156

Restaurants

Duane's Prime Steak's (3649
Mission Inn Avenue), 153, 155
Mission Inn Restaurant (3649
Mission Inn Avenue), 155
Simple Simon's (3639 Main
Street), 154

Attractions

Fox Theater (3801 Mission Inn
Avenue), 155
Glen Ivy Hot Springs Spa
(25000 Glen Ivy Road), 153,
156
Mission Inn Museum (3649
Mission Inn Avenue), 154
Perris Valley Skydiving (2091
Goetz Road), 156
Riverside Film Festival, 156

Activities

Carriage House (3491 Market
Street), 153, 154

ROSARITO, MEXICO

Lodging

La Fonda (Highway 1-D,
Kilometer 39), 7, 129, 130
Rosarito Beach Hotel (Benito
Juarez Boulevard), 128, 129

Restaurants

Chabert's Gourmet Dining
Restaurant and Steakhouse
(Rosarito Beach Hotel), 128,
130
La Fonda (Highway 1-D,
Kilometer 39), 7, 129, 130
La Casa de Langosta (Puerto
Nuevo), 132
Lobster House (Puerto Nuevo),
132

Attractions

Bajamar Golf Course, 132
Casa Playa Spa (Benito Juarez
Boulevard), 128, 131
Fox Baja Film Studios, 130
Real del Mar Golf Course, 132

General Index